Differentiated Instruction for World Languages

With Student-Centered Projects

Toolkit for Foreign Language Teachers

Sue Hubbert

Taru Nieminen

Differentiated Instruction for World Languages

With Student-Centered Projects

Levels I & II

Sue Hubbert, M.A. and Taru Nieminen, M.A.T.

Library of Congress Cataloging-in-Publication Data

Differentiated Instruction for world languages with student-centered projects. /Sue Hubbert and Taru Nieminen

ISBN 978-0-9889791-2-3

1. World language— Study and teaching. 2. Foreign language— Study and teaching.

3. Differentiated instruction. 4. Curriculum. 5. Assessment and rubrics.

Copyright ©2013 Hubbert and Nieminen

Edited by Sue Hubbert and Taru Nieminen

Layout and design by Taru Nieminen and Kristiina Gray

Cover Layout by Ashley Kasul

ISBN 978-0-9889791-2-3

The purchase of this book entitles the buyer to reproduce the activities and assessment rubric pages for classroom use only. All rights reserved. This book may not be reproduced, transmitted, or stored in whole or in part by any means, including graphic, electronic, or mechanical without the express written consent of the authors except in the case of brief quotations embodied in critical articles and reviews. For information regarding permission, please write to Sue Hubbert and Taru Nieminen via e-mail with the subject line of: **WLT Permissions** at WLToolkit@gmail.com.

At the time of publication, all websites and other factual content are the most current available. All URLs are accurate and active. The authors make no warranty or guarantee concerning the information and materials given out by organizations or content found at web sites. The authors are not responsible for any changes that occur after the publication of this book. If you find an error, please contact the authors at WLToolkit@gmail.com.

Our toolkit includes engaging, supplementary activities to foster critical thinking, creativity, responsibility, and independence in a foreign language classroom.

- Teaching tips included with each section!
- Aligned to national standards- each activity coded for easy transition into your lesson plans!
- An assessment rubric is provided with each activity sheet- grading is a snap!
- Each unit contains supplementary projects to create and nurture an exciting learning environment for your world language learners!

We hope you and your students enjoy these lessons as much as we do!

Sincerely,

Sue Hubbert and Taru Nieminen

©2013 Hubbert and Nieminen

Table of Contents

Introduction

- The Why and the How 1
- Teacher Tips for Successful Projects 2
- Student Tips and Responsibilities 4
- National Standards and Benefits of Second Language Learning 5

Unit 1: Getting Started

A

- Teacher Tips Page for Section A 8
- Alphabet 9
- Names and Nametags 11
- Numbers and Money 13
- Expressing Time 15

B

- Teacher Tips Page for Section B 17
- Dates, Days of the Week, and Months 18
- Seasons and Weather 20
- Greetings, Responses, and Introductions 22
- Colors and Clothing 24

C

- Teacher Tips Page for Section C 26
- Classroom Objects 27
- School Subjects, Teachers, and Times 29
- Family Nouns 31

Unit 2: Connecting with Culture

- ❖ Teacher Tips for Pages 35 to 42 34
- ❖ General Heritage and Customs 35
- ❖ Customs and Traditions 37
- ❖ Family Life 39
- ❖ Foods 41
- ❖ Teacher Tips for Pages 44 to 51 43
- ❖ Traditional Clothing 44
- ❖ Modern Clothing 46
- ❖ Arts and Education 48
- ❖ Famous People 50

Unit 3: Home and Abroad

- ❖ Teacher Tips Page for Unit 3 53
- ❖ House and Home 54
- ❖ Neighborhood and Directions 56
- ❖ City and Transportation 58

Unit 4: Body and Mind

- ❖ Teacher Tips Page for Unit 4 61
- ❖ Parts of the Body 62
- ❖ Sports and Hobbies 64
- ❖ Feelings and Emotions 66
- ❖ Technology 68

Unit 5: Score with Grammar

- Teacher Tips for Pages 72 to 79 71
- Nouns 72
- Adjectives 74
- Pronouns: Formal and Informal 76
- Verbs 78
- Teacher Tips for Pages 81 to 84 80
- Exclamations, Questions, and Declarative Sentences 81
- Likes and Dislikes 83

Unit 6: Going Places

- Teacher Tips for Pages 88 to 95 87
- Going to the Market 88
- Choose Your Ticket: Sporting Events, Concerts, Bus and Train Rides 90
- Vacation and Travel 92
- Visiting or Obtaining Services from Community Service Programs 94
- Teacher Tips for Pages 97 to 103 96
- Shopping Experience 97
- Eating Out 99
- Public and Private Schools 102

Reference Pages and Templates

- Teacher Tips for Pages 106-114 105
- Shopping List 106
- Facts and Figures 107
- Commands 108
- Clock template 109
- Facebook Page template 110
- Race for the Numbers 112
- Bingo Chart template 113
- More VERB activities 114

Introduction

❖ The Why and the How

Why?
- ❖ We need to produce leaders who are creative, critical, and independent thinkers
- ❖ Latest research reveals the effectiveness of Student-Centered teaching and Project-Based learning
- ❖ Differentiated Instruction allows each student to achieve his/her level of development and success
- ❖ Projects allow students to work at their own levels
- ❖ Ready-made assessments with rubrics support Common-Core Standards
- ❖ Student assignments are required to meet cross-curricular standards

This Book:
- ❖ Aligns to National Standards for Learning Languages
- ❖ Fits into the Project-Based Learning format
- ❖ Challenges the unique learning styles of each student
- ❖ Encourages more mature language acquisition
- ❖ Offers many projects with cross-curricular standards
- ❖ Provides the learner with Student-Centered and Student-Generated projects

How?
- ❖ Teachers give the students the suggestion of an *idea* which sparks critical and innovative thinking instead of word-for-word instruction
- ❖ The students' determination of *how* to use the information is crucial to the creation of the Einsteins and Edisons of the next generation
- ❖ The projects keep all work student centered and student generated
- ❖ Students are empowered when given the reins to direct their own learning
- ❖ Teachers can easily recognize the connection between the activity and the National Standard it supports

This Book:
- ❖ Facilitates the inclusion of standards into the teachers' lesson plans
- ❖ Provides teacher tips for activities which spark critical and innovative thinking
- ❖ Generates independent thinkers
- ❖ Allows students to make integral decisions to achieve project success
- ❖ Builds on the Three Modes of Communication and independent study
- ❖ Provides different language situations through realistic interactions

❖ Teacher Tips for Successful Projects

- ❖ Have students use the target language as much as possible to complete projects.
- ❖ To effectively use the target language, most projects have a requirement for a presentation element to class or teacher. Adjustments may be necessary to achieve the desired student outcome.
- ❖ If you have time constraints to showcase student projects, split students into groups and have each student within a group present his/her project. This enables you to go around the room to listen, watch, and assess.
- ❖ Displaying and presenting projects gives students a sense of accomplishment and pride.
- ❖ When students complete "Your Choice" projects, it is their responsibility to write down assessment requirements for your approval. Students should write these in the rubric square provided.
- ❖ Unless otherwise noted, students are expected to use color in all the projects. There are only a few exceptions. Research has proven that COLOR stimulates and inspires creativity! ☺
- ❖ In the projects, "as close to scale as possible" means appropriate size within the project, i.e. all elements must correspond in size and distance.
- ❖ Because of the creative nature of the projects, please ensure that students understand the *required* elements of the projects.
- ❖ Since every teacher, classroom, and group of students are unique, please feel free to add or remove any elements of the assessments to adapt to your particular situation.
- ❖ **Menus:**
    - **Tic-tac-toe**: Students choose 3 in a row; diagonal, across or down.
    - **Nine-Square Menu**: Students choose two to complete.
    - **Columns**: Students complete one from Column I and one more from Columns II or III.
    - **Score 100**: Instructions are on the project sheet.
    - **List menu**: Instructions are on the project sheet.
- ❖ **Teacher's Choice Projects:**
    - Excellent group projects.
    - Teacher chooses groups.
    - Teacher assigns project(s) for each group.
    - Teacher gives groups a time limit on presentation.
    - Group presents its project together; all members must be part of presentation.
    - Projects make great displays for the classroom.
    - OPTIONAL: Have each group come up with 2-3 questions about their topic which the teacher then transfers onto a worksheet for students to complete as a quiz.
    - TECHNOLOGY IS FABULOUS: Teachers have students email the questions to them which they then proofread, copy, and paste to a document: quiz created. ☺
- ❖ **Easy Grading for *Score 100* menu**:

This menu requires students to select one or more projects which add up to 100. To keep the assessment simple, the rubrics use the same point value (25) as all others. To calculate final grade for each student, determine the percentage of points earned.

EXAMPLE 1: Student A has chosen the 20, 30, and 50 *Score 100*-projects from the menu. Student A has received 60 out of 75 on the assessment rubrics. To determine overall percentage, divide 60 by 75. The student has earned an 80% for a grade.

EXAMPLE 2: Student B has chosen the 20 and 80 *Score 100*-projects and has received a total of 45 out of 50 on the assessment rubrics. Divide 45 by 50; student has earned a 90%

- ❖ **How to define *creativity* as an assessment?** In several projects, we have included "Creativity counts" as an assessment piece. Below are the dictionary definitions for the words *creative, original,* and *imagination.*
    - *Creative*: 1. Characterized by originality; 2. Imaginative.
    - *Original*: 1. Initial, first; 2. Fresh and unusual, new; 3. Creative, inventive.
    - *Imagination*: 1. The process or power of forming a mental image of something not real or present; 2. Creativity, inventiveness; 3. Resourcefulness.
- ❖ **Take something that is known, and give it a fresh approach, as in the following examples:**
    - A kite is designed to hang in the room. One girl's kite is a tuxedo. A boy's kite is shaped like a basketball.
    - A game is created with a painted pizza box as a game board and container "all in one."
    - A PowerPoint is designed with a fresh approach to share the information. E.g. music, animation, or graphics are innovatively added.
    - A song is composed with original lyrics and score.
- ❖ **Challenges**
    - Use as additional individual projects or as extra credit projects.
- ❖ **We recommend you have the following items on hand in order to complete most of the projects:**
    - Poster board, glue, glue gun, tape, markers, colored pencils, white copy paper, 8.5 x 11 in. and 12 x 18 in. construction paper, scissors, old magazines of all kinds, magazines in the target language, yarn, string, paper fasteners/brads, paper punch, rulers.
    - Shopping list of items provided in the *Reference Pages and Templates* section.

- ❖ **How to bind books:**
    - Staple the sheets of paper down the middle of the book with an oversized book stapler.
    - Paper-punch holes (min. 2 required) in the side of the book and lace them together.
    - Paper-punch and use individual rings, bag ties, wire, etc. to tie the book together.
    - Fold and staple along the spine (min. 2 staples).
    - Sew along spine with sewing machine or use yarn.
    - Use brass fasteners to keep book together.
    - Make sure that sharp ends of staples are covered with tape or glue.
- ❖ **How to make flipbooks:**
    Here are a few websites we found:
    - http://www.readwritethink.org/files/resources/interactives/flipbook/ (You are able to type the titles, draw, type text onto the pages, and print the book!)
    - http://pinterest.com/sjww/teacher-made-books/ (Many types of different books to make.)
    - YouTube videos: https://www.youtube.com/watch?v=4N0X3DkXNtM and https://www.youtube.com/watch?v=S824yY9ZeqM.

❖ Student Tips and Responsibilities for Successful Projects

- ❖ The purpose is to connect you to the target language.
- ❖ Use the target language to complete projects whenever possible.
- ❖ For "Your Choice," it is your responsibility to write down the requirements for the project, which your teacher will then approve. (Hint: Write them down first on a separate sheet, so your teacher can make suggestions or corrections and then transfer them to the rubric.)
- ❖ Remember to keep a copy of the rubric so the teacher can use it to grade your project(s).
- ❖ In the projects, "as close to scale as possible" means appropriate size within the project; all elements should correspond in size and distance. For example, people should not be larger than a building.
- ❖ All illustrations should be in color. To accomplish this requirement, use markers/colored pencils/paints, magazine pictures, photos, pictures from the internet, and/or clipart. There are only a few exceptions to this requirement.
- ❖ Since every teacher, classroom, and student is unique, please be aware that your teacher may add or remove any element of the assessment.
- ❖ Almost all projects require you to use the target language during your presentation(s); after all, that's why you are taking this class. ☺
- ❖ Keep a journal to jot down ideas for future projects.
- ❖ **Here are some things you can start to collect for future projects:**
    - Shoeboxes and other boxes appropriate for "diorama" size
    - Poster board, large pieces of cardboard
    - Scrapbook materials
    - Old magazines

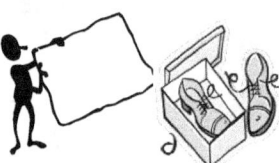

- ❖ **How to bind books:**
    - Staple the sheets of paper down the middle of the book with an oversized book stapler.
    - Paper-punch holes (min. 2 required) in the side of the book and lace them together.
    - Paper-punch and use individual rings, bag ties, wire, etc. to tie the book together.
    - Fold and staple along the spine (min. 2 staples).
    - Sew along spine with sewing machine or use yarn.
    - Use brass fasteners to keep book together.
    - Make sure that sharp ends of staples are covered with tape or glue.
- ❖ **Interesting Facts about Language**
    - Korean is the only language which has a known origin.
    - Chinese, Japanese, and Finnish are the three hardest languages to learn in the world. They compete for first place amongst each other in most polls taken.
    - English: What other words besides "hungry" and "angry" end in "-gry?" There aren't any!
    - The United Nations uses six official languages to conduct business: English, French, Spanish, Chinese, Russian and Arabic.[1]
    - It's estimated that up to 7,000 different languages are spoken around the world.[2]
    - Pinocchio is Italian for "pine eye."
    - Eskimoes have hundreds of words for "ice" but none for "hello."[3]
    - In nearly every language around the world, the word for "mother" begins with an *m* sound. Some exceptions can be found in the Uralic language group (e.g. äiti in Finnish.)[4]

---

[1] http://www.bbc.co.uk/languages/guide/languages.shtml
[2] http://www.bbc.co.uk/languages/guide/languages.shtml
[3] http://www.rcasteel.com/StrangeThings/language.aspx
[4] http://www.allfunandgames.ca/facts/languages.shtml

❖ National Standards for Foreign Language Learning (U.S.)

Each project has been tagged with one of the national standards; however, many of the projects meet more than one national standard when completed by the student. Many projects also meet various cross-curricular standards.

STANDARDS FOR FOREIGN LANGUAGE LEARNING can be found on the American Council on the Teaching of Foreign Languages website: http://www.actfl.org/ and further in their publication: National Standards for Foreign Language Education.

❖ ASSESSMENT

Based on the National Standards

- The "Teacher Tips" pages for each section or unit contain the National Standards for each of the student projects.
- The format of the National Standards diagram corresponds to the assessment rubric format for each project sheet. Example below.

Alphabet Assessment Rubric

*Write an Acrostic Poem ___/5	*Make Flashcards ___/5	*Create Word Search ___/5
*Lead a Spelling Bee ___/5	*Your Choice! ___/5	*Design a Game ___/5
*Write an Alphabet Book ___/5	*Draw an Alphabet People Poster ___/5	*Compose a Song or a Rap ___/5

Corresponding National Standards

Alphabet

1.2	1.2	1.2
1.2		1.3
1.3	3.1/Art	1.3

Differentiated Instruction for World Languages ©2013 Hubbert and Nieminen

❖ Share the Benefits of Learning a Foreign Language with your students.

Second language study:
- ❖ Benefits academic progress in other subjects
- ❖ Narrows achievement gaps
- ❖ Benefits basic skills development
- ❖ Benefits higher order, abstract and creative thinking
- ❖ Enhances a student's sense of achievement
- ❖ Helps students score higher on standardized tests
- ❖ Promotes cultural awareness and competency
- ❖ Improves chances of college acceptance, achievement and attainment
- ❖ Enhances career opportunities
- ❖ Benefits understanding and security in community and society
- ❖ Early second language study enriches and enhances cognitive development

*Regarding World Language Education
 NEA Research, December 2007
 http://www.sde.ct.gov/sde/lib/sde/PDF/Curriculum/Curriculum_Root_Web_Folder/BenefitsofSecondLanguage.pdf

Notes:

Unit 1: Getting Started

A
- Teacher Tips Page for Section A 8
- Alphabet 9
- Names and Nametags 11
- Numbers and Money 13
- Expressing Time 15

B
- Teacher Tips Page for Section B 17
- Dates, Days of the Week, and Months 18
- Seasons and Weather 20
- Greetings, Responses, and Introductions 22
- Colors and Clothing 24

C
- Teacher Tips Page for Section C 26
- Classroom Objects 27
- School Subjects, Teachers, and Times 29
- Family Nouns 31

Teacher Tips Page for Section A

Standards

Alphabet

1.2	1.2	1.2
1.2		1.3
1.3	3.1/Art	1.3

➢ **Challenge**: 1.1

Names and Nametags

All projects
3.2

Numbers and Money

2.2	1.3	1.3
3.1		3.1/Math
1.3	4.1	1.3

Time

1.1	1.3	4.2
1.3		4.1/Tech
1.2	1.3	2.1

➢ **Challenge**: 1.1

❖ **Preview Material**
  o For videotaped or recorded products, it is always wise to preview the video or recording prior to class presentation.

❖ **Alphabet**
  o Example for Alphabet Acrostic in English:
    Affirming
    Literate
    Practical
    Hip and happening
    Accurate
    Beautiful
    Entertaining
    Terrific

❖ **Numbers and Money**
  o For easy conversion tables and a universal currency converter, use http://www.xe.com/.

❖ **Time**
  o Make copies of Facebook Page template on page 110-111.

The Alphabet

Select "Three-in-a-Row" to complete the tic-tac-toe.

Write an Acrostic Poem	Make Flashcards	Create a Word Search
Write an acrostic poem for the word alphabet in the target language using vocabulary words.	Design letters to illustrate each letter/character of the alphabet. May be completed with a partner.	Create a word search with every letter/character of the alphabet in the target language.
Lead a Spelling Bee	**Your Choice!**	**Design a Game**
Use current vocabulary words or student names to put on a spelling bee for your classmates.		Design a game using the alphabet; e.g. "Around the World."
Write an Alphabet Book	**Create an Alphabet People Poster**	**Write and Perform a Song or a Rap**
Write and illustrate an alphabet book in the target language.	Create a poster of "Alphabet People."	Write and perform an original song or rap using the alphabet.

➢ **Challenge**: <u>Shoot a Video</u> of yourself teaching/learning the alphabet in the target language.

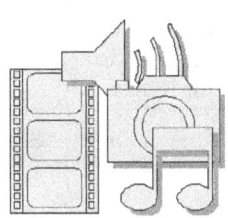

Shoot a Video	
* Taped for teacher review	___ / 5
* Must include all letters of target language alphabet	___ / 5
* Clear pronunciation and adequate volume	___ / 5
* Show off your talents creatively	___ / 5
* Perform live or play video	___ / 5
Total points	___ / 25

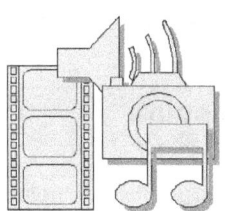

Alphabet Assessment Rubric

Write an Acrostic Poem		Make Flashcards		Create a Word Search	
* Min. 8.5 x 11 in.	/5	* Max. 4 x 6 in. index card	/5	* Min. 8.5 x 11 in.	/5
* Each descriptive word/phrase chosen must begin with one of the letters from the target word	/5	* Must include an object which begins with specific letter	/5	* Must include a min. of 20 vocabulary words	/5
* Typed or neatly written with target word aligned on the side of the paper	/5	* Label each object on the reverse side of the card	/5	* Each word must start with a different letter of the alphabet	/5
* Use color	/5	* Cards must be in a container or carrying bag	/5	* Include answer key and puzzle	/5
* Illustrate your poem	/5	* Present to class	/5	* Neatly written or typed	/5
Total points	/25	**Total points**	/25	**Total Points**	/25

Lead a Spelling Bee		_____!		Design a Game	
*Min. 20 words/names	/5		/5	* Must include 20 questions or activity cards	/5
* Each word/name written on half a sheet of paper	/5		/5	* Include thematic title	/5
* Neatly printed words	/5		/5	* Complete set of rules	/5
* Prepare a certificate for winner(s)	/5		/5	* Devise a written plan for teams and order of participation	/5
* Lead the spelling bee	/5		/5	* Lead the game	/5
Total points	/25	**Total points**	/25	**Total points**	/25

Write an Alphabet Book		Create an Alphabet People Poster		Write and Perform a Song or Rap	
* Min. 5 x 7 in.	/5	* Standard poster size	/5	* Perform live or play video	/5
* Illustrated front and back covers	/5	* Each letter designed with different " font " people	/5	* Each letter of the target language alphabet must be included	/5
* Include entire alphabet	/5	* Must have imaginative title	/5	* Must have melody	/5
* Illustrate in color	/5	* Must be in color	/5	* Must be sung in alphabetical order	/5
* Authors' name on front cover	/5	* Name on the back	/5	* Taped/written copy of words to teacher prior to performance for review	/5
Total points	/25	**Total points**	/25	**Total points**	/25

Show your project choices to your teacher by: _____

All of your projects are due on: _____

Names and Nametags

A complete language experience calls for the student to immerse herself into the target language. What better way than to require the students to pick a new target language first name for themselves. This should be accomplished within the first week of the class, preferably in the first three days. Doing this has proven to be very effective for student involvement.

How to make nametags:

- **Items needed:**
    - Poster board or heavy cardboard
    - Markers, pens, pencils, colored pencils
    - String/yarn
- **Directions:**
    - Cut the board to about 4 x 11 in. size (this is big enough to see from across the room, as students need to learn each other's names!)
    - Students write their new first names onto cardboard and illustrate with pictures that tell about them.

Activities for students/teacher to learn new names:

- Introduce oneself in the target language.
- "My name is…" game. Items needed: nametags and a ball or other soft object to throw.
    - Say "My name is…" in the target language, then…
    - Say someone else's name and toss the ball to that person.
    - The person to whom you throw the ball says "My name is…." and so on.
    - It is important that the ball reaches everyone in the room: a student may not toss the ball to someone who has already had a turn.
- Same activity as the "My name is…" game, but the ball gets passed to the person right next to you and so on. This is a faster version if you are pressed for time or just need a quick activity for an end or start of the class.
- Teacher instructs students to whom to throw the ball. Great activity for the teacher to learn the students' new names.
- After the 2nd day with nametags, have students flip their nametags (or put them away) for the last couple of rounds of any of the games and then start the "My name is…." game.
- Spelling Bee with student names. Each correctly spelled name receives a point/ reward.
- Students write names on the board. Teacher gives points to each correctly spelled name.

Continues on next page

- ❖ **Name Quiz:**
    - Students sit in their desks.
    - Each student has a large number on a piece of paper fastened to the front of his/her desk.
    - Give each student a "quiz" paper with number of students in class, e.g. 1-25.
    - Students write each student's name on corresponding line.

OR

    - Teacher provides a list of names to match or to rewrite names on the line.

Make a Nametag	
* Approx. 4 x 11 in.	____/5
* Use heavy paper or cardboard	____/5
* Name spelled correctly	____/5
* Must use color	____/5
* Creativity counts	____/5
Total points	____/ 25

Handmade

Computer generated

Numbers and Money

Select "Three-in-a-Row" to complete the tic-tac-toe.

Make a List	Create a Game	Design a Picture Book
Make a list of at least 10 items in your room at home using the target language's monetary units.	Create a game with numbers using the target language.	Design a picture book of numbers with pictures and labels.
Perform a Cheer Choreograph and perform a cheer. You may use video to showcase your talent. 	**Your Choice!** 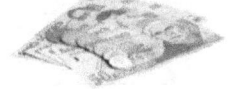	**Create a Worksheet** Create a worksheet using the numbers 1-100. 
Design a Poster Design a poster with at least 10 items labeled with a price in the target language monetary units. Call on classmates to express the cost in the target language.	**Make Flashcards** Make flashcards with the written number on the back of the flashcard in the target language and the numeral on the other.	**Create a Crossword Puzzle** Create a crossword puzzle. The answers are the solutions to the number problems. Solutions must be in the target language.

Numbers and Money Assessment Rubric

Make a List		Create a Game		Design a Picture Book	
* Min. 10 items	____/5	* Min. 20 question/activity cards	____/5	* Min. 5 x 7 in., bound	____/5
* Illustrate in color or cut pictures from magazines	____/5	* Include a thematic title for your game	____/5	* Min. 10 pages or 25 numbers	____/5
* Prices must be appropriate	____/5	* Include complete set of rules	____/5	* Illustrate in color (drawings, magazine or internet pictures)	____/5
* Label each item	____/5	* Devise a plan for teams and order of participation	____/5	* Label each illustration	____/5
* Present to class	____/5	* Lead the game	____/5	* Read your book to the class	____/5
Total points	____/25	**Total points**	____/25	**Total Points**	____/25
Perform a Cheer		**_____!**		**Create a Worksheet**	
* Min. 1 minute in length	____/5		____/5	* Typed or neatly written	____/5
* Include 20 target elements	____/5		____/5	* Include addition and subtraction problems	____/5
* Record for teacher review prior to performance	____/5		____/5	* Number range 1-100	____/5
* Includes at least one other person	____/5		____/5	* Solution must be 100 or less	____/5
* Perform live or play video	____/5		____/5	* Include answer key	____/5
Total points	____/25	**Total points**	____/25	**Total points**	____/25
Design a Poster		**Make Flashcards**		**Create a Crossword Puzzle**	
* Standard poster size	____/5	* 3 x 5 in. index cards	____/5	* Min. 20 clues	____/5
* Min. 10 items labeled	____/5	* Min. 25 cards with container/carrying bag	____/5	* Develop appropriate clues using numerals	____/5
* Prices must be appropriate	____/5	* Solution must be 100 or less	____/5	* Solution must be written in target language	____/5
* Call on classmates to express the cost in the target language	____/5	* Number problem on one side, solution on the other	____/5	* 3 classmates must solve puzzle (turn in completed/corrected puzzles)**	____/5
* Illustrate in color (drawings, magazine or internet pictures)	____/5	* Play the game with a partner	____/5	* Include puzzle and answer key	____/5
Total points	____/25	**Total points**	____/25	**Total points**	____/25

Show your project choices to your teacher by: _____

All of your projects are due on: _____

**Ask teacher to make copies

Differentiated Instruction for World Languages ©2013 Hubbert and Nieminen

Expressing Time

Select "Three-in-a-Row" to complete the tic-tac-toe.

Make Flashcards	Create a Poster	Design a Flipbook
Make flashcards with the clock on one side and the correct phrase in the target language on the other.	Design a large clock poster to illustrate and teach the time expressions in the target language.	Create a flipbook with clock faces on the front and the correct expression in the target language on the inside.
Design a Picture Book Write and design a picture book with illustrations expressing what the character(s) do at different times during the day.	**Your Choice!** 	**Update Facebook** "Update" your status informing your friends about your plans on Saturday. You are very busy! List 10 activities and the times using the target language.
Write a Diary Entry Tell your diary about your daily schedule at school: what you do (classes and activities) and when.	**Perform a Dialogue** Create a dialogue in the target language expressing the times of different activities. Perform the dialogue with a classmate.	**Create Airline Schedules** Recreate an airline schedule on a large poster detailing the arrivals and departures of different flights in a country that speaks your target language.

➢ **Challenge**: <u>Create a Schedule</u> of your family activities for an entire week.

Create a Schedule	
* Use target language time expressions	____ / 5
* Min. two entries per day for one week	____ / 5
* Neatly written in appropriate format	____ / 5
* Use color and illustrations	____ / 5
* Present to class in an imaginative way	____ / 5
Total points	____ / 25

Expressing Time Assessment Rubric

Make Flashcards		Create a Poster		Design a Flipbook	
* 3 x 5 in. index cards	___/5	* Standard poster size, use both sides of poster	___/5	* Min. 8.5 x 11 in., folded in half	___/5
* Min. 20 different expressions of time	___/5	* All expressions of time must be included, min. 20	___/5	* 10 expressions of time	___/5
* Clock on one side, correct phrase in target language on the other	___/5	* Clocks can be drawn free hand or made from cut-outs /computer generated	___/5	* Time elements must be in correct form in the target language	___/5
* Include container or carrying bag for cards	___/5	* Illustrate in color	___/5	* Illustrate in color	___/5
* Play the game with a partner	___/5	* Teach to class or group	___/5	* Neatly written and drawn or computer generated	___/5
Total points	___/25	**Total points**	___/25	**Total Points**	___/25

Design a Picture Book		_____!		Update Facebook	
* Min. 5 x 7 in., bound	___/5		___/5	* Use Facebook template	___/5
* Min. 10 pages	___/5		___/5	* Include 10 activities using complete sentences	___/5
* Cover with title and author (student) name	___/5		___/5	* All entries in target language	___/5
* Use complete sentences in target language	___/5		___/5	* Copy of printed page to teacher for review	___/5
* Illustrations in color (drawings, magazine or internet pictures)	___/5		___/5	* Present to class	___/5
Total points	___/25	**Total points**	___/25	**Total points**	___/25

Write a Diary Entry		Perform a Dialogue		Create Airline Schedules	
* Min. 10 entries of activities/ classes	___/5	* Neatly written or typed; one copy for you, one for teacher review	___/5	* Neatly written or typed	___/5
* Min. 10 time expressions included	___/5	* Correct use of grammar and time structure	___/5	* Include min. 5 arrivals and 5 departures	___/5
* Give your entries a cohesive title	___/5	* Min. 10 lines using complete sentences	___/5	* Use actual city names	___/5
* Use the 1st person for entries	___/5	* Min. of 5 time expressions	___/5	* Include two out-of-country flights	___/5
* Neatly written or typed	___/5	* Perform to class	___/5	* Must be in color with appropriate layout	___/5
Total points	___/25	**Total points**	___/25	**Total points**	___/25

Show your project choices to your teacher by: _____

All of your projects are due on: _____

Teacher Tips Page for Section B

Standards

Expressing Dates, Days of the Week, and Months

1.3	1.1	1.3
4.2		1.3
1.3	3.1/Art	1.1

➢ **Challenge:** 4.1

Seasons and Weather

3.1/Science	2.1	3.2
3.2		4.1
4.1	3.1/Science	1.3

➢ **Challenge:** 3.1/Science

Greetings, Responses and Introductions

All projects		
1.1	1.2	1.3

Colors and Clothing

1.3	1.1	3.1/Music
1.1		3.1/Tech
1.1	1.1	1.2

➢ **Challenge 1:** 3.1
➢ **Challenge 2:** 3.2

❖ **Preview Material**
  o For videotaped or recorded products, it is always wise to preview the video or recording prior to class presentation.
❖ **Expressing Dates, Days of the Week, and Months**
  o Ideas for "Your Choice": Design T-shirts or socks for each day of the week or months of the year, draw a comic strip of goofy activities for each day of the week or each month of the year.
❖ Use **Greetings, Responses, and Introductions** assessment for a test! ☺
❖ **Colors and Clothing**
  o Give bonus points for "creative" thinkers, e.g. using target country fashions in projects.
❖ **Seasons and Weather**
  ➢ **Extra Challenge:** Construct a Diorama. Build and label a diorama of the four seasons (or your favorite season) in the target language country. Write a paragraph in the target language describing your diorama.   **Challenge:** 1.3 /Science

Construct a Diorama	
* Min. 1 shoebox size (or approx. 5x14x16)	____ / 5
* Min. five 3-D objects	____ / 5
* All surfaces decorated	____ / 5
* Appropriate title	____ / 5
* Paragraph with 5-6 sentences	____ / 5
Total points	____ / 25

Dates, Days of the Week, Months of the Year

Select "Three-in-a-Row" to complete the tic-tac-toe.

Create a Photo-folio	Organize a Survey Chart	Design a Poster
Illustrate two activities for each day of the week using the target language. 	Organize a survey chart with classmate birthdays. You need to interview each one to get your information.	Design a poster with the four seasons. Draw or use magazine/online photos and include each month for each season.
Create a Calendar	Your Choice!	Create a Word Search
Create a calendar in the target language for the next year with illustrations for each month.		Create a word search using days of the week and months of the year vocabulary.
List Family Birthdays	Create a Craft Activity	Create a Timeline
Verbally indicate the birthdays of your immediate family and close friends.	Create a craft activity incorporating target vocabulary.	Create a timeline of your family's important events during one calendar year. Can be in 3-D. 

➢ **Challenge:** Create a Children's Book using the song "Monday is the day we wash our clothes..." as you incorporate the target language vocabulary.

Create a Children's Book	
* Min. 5 x 7 in., bound	____ / 5
* Min. 14 activities, min. one for each day of the week	____ / 5
* Write a descriptive sentence for each activity	____ / 5
* Day of the week labeled prominently	____ / 5
* Illustrate in color (may be stick figures)	____ / 5
Total points	____ / 25

Differentiated Instruction for World Languages ©2013 Hubbert and Nieminen

Dates, Days, Months of the Year Assessment Rubric

Create a Photo-folio		Organize a Survey Chart		Design a Poster	
* Min. 5 x 7 in., bound	/5	* Ask a min. of 12 people	/5	* Standard poster size	/5
* Min. 14 activities	/5	* Interview and answers must be in target language	/5	* Illustrations in color (drawings, magazine or internet pictures)	/5
* Write a descriptive sentence for each activity	/5	*Organize chart by months; include all 12 months	/5	* Months and seasons labeled	/5
* Day of the week labeled prominently	/5	* Illustrate in color	/5	* Title your poster	/5
* Illustrate in color (may be stick figures)	/5	* Share results with class using target language	/5	* Must be neat and legible with correct spelling	/5
Total points	**/ 25**	**Total points**	**/ 25**	**Total Points**	**/ 25**

Create a Calendar		_____!		Create a Word Search	
* Neatly written or computer generated with correct spelling	/5		/5	* Neatly written or typed	/5
* Include all the months of the year and days of the week	/5		/5	* Include all days of the week and months of the year	/5
* Must include major holidays of target country	/5		/5	* Have three classmates solve the puzzle and turn in corrected puzzles **	/5
* Illustrate in color	/5		/5	* Use shape and color to enhance the word search	/5
* Must be for the next calendar year	/5		/5	* Include puzzle and answer key	/5
Total points	**/ 25**	**Total points**	**/ 25**	**Total points**	**/ 25**

List Family Birthdays		Create a Craft Activity		Create a Timeline	
* Neatly written or typed in the target language	/5	* Neatly written or typed with illustration(s) of craft	/5	* No larger than 3 ft. long, 1 ft. high	/5
* Include min. 10 family members/ friends	/5	* Title your craft activity	/5	* Min. 12 events on the calendar with a brief explanation for each	/5
* Include relation to you	/5	* Include complete instruction sheet with illustrations	/5	* Dates must be indicated in the target language	/5
* Include sketch or photo of each person in color	/5	* Test your instruction sheet as a classmate creates the craft	/5	* Must have a colored illustration or 3-D object beside each date/event	/5
* Present to class	/5	* Create the craft to show as an example	/5	* Present to class	/5
Total points	**/ 25**	**Total points**	**/ 25**	**Total points**	**/ 25**

Show your project choices to your teacher by: _____

All of your projects are due on: _____

**Ask your teacher to make copies

Differentiated Instruction for World Languages ©2013 Hubbert and Nieminen

Seasons and Weather

Select two projects to complete.

Construct a Mobile	Organize a Flipbook	Design a Brochure
Create a mobile with the seasons in the target country. Include descriptions of the seasons. 	Organize a flipbook of seasonal activities for your target country. Inside each flap, illustrate and label at least two activities for the season using target vocabulary.	Design a colorful brochure for a resort in the country that speaks the target language. Include seasonal and weather information for the resort area.
Create a Poster Create a poster with the four seasons and the type of weather that the target country would have during each season.	 Your Choice!	**Write an Acrostic Poem** Write an acrostic poem for at least two seasons using the target language adjectives.
Sort into a Venn Diagram Compare and contrast yours and the target country's seasons and/or weather. Suggested comparisons: clothing, temperatures, activities, weather patterns/zones, etc.	**Research and Illustrate** Research the types of weather phenomena in a country that speaks the target language. Illustrate the phenomenon and use the target language's term(s) to label each picture.	**Create a Card Game** Create a card game with seasons and weather terms in the target language. 

> **Challenge:** Research Different Weather Terms. Illustrate and label the weather terms in the target language in a format of your choice. Write a sentence or two describing the weather terms.

Research Weather Terms	
* Use target language	___ / 5
* Illustrations in color	___ / 5
* Separate bibliography	___ / 5
* Appropriate format selected	___ / 5
* Present to class in an imaginative way	___ / 5
Total points	___ / 25

Seasons and Weather Assessment Rubric

Construct a Mobile		Organize a Flipbook		Design a Brochure	
* Min. 10 pieces of written information in target language	/5	* Min. 8.5 x 11 in., folded	/5	* Min. 8.5 x 11 in., folded	/5
* Illustrations must be in color	/5	* Name of season on front flap	/5	* Include seasonal and weather information	/5
* Min. 3 layers of mobile elements	/5	* Include and label all four seasons	/5	* Must have both pictures and written information	/5
* Must be balanced	/5	* Two labeled, seasonal activities for each season under each flap	/5	* Neatly written or computer generated	/5
* Show and tell to class	/5	* Illustrate in color	/5	* Creativity counts	/5
Total points	/25	**Total points**	/25	**Total Points**	/25
Create a Poster		_____!		Write an Acrostic Poem	
* Standard poster size	/5		/5	* Min. 8.5 x 11 in.	/5
* Illustrations in color (drawings, magazine or internet pictures)	/5		/5	* Neatly written or typed with word aligned on side of paper	/5
* Use target language	/5		/5	* Each word must be descriptive	/5
* Write description for weather and label seasons	/5		/5	* Illustrate your poem	/5
* Include name of target country in title	/5		/5	* Use color	/5
Total points	/25	**Total points**	/25	**Total points**	/25
Sort into a Venn Diagram		Research and Illustrate		Create a Card Game	
* Min. 8.5 x 11 in.	/5	* Include research in a separate bibliography	/5	* Cards are 3 x 5 in. size	/5
* Title of Venn including sets that are relevant	/5	* Illustrations in color	/5	* Min. 20 cards or amount necessary to play the game	/5
* Must be neatly drawn	/5	* Label pictures	/5	* One side decorated with illustration(s) in color and with name of game	/5
* Min. 12 items in target language	/5	* Include weather zone map for the target country	/5	* Typed instructions on how to play are included	/5
* Use color to enhance your Venn Diagram	/5	* Select appropriate medium to display your results	/5	* Include container or carrying bag for cards	/5
Total points	/25	**Total points**	/25	**Total points**	/25

Show your project choices to your teacher by: _____

All of your projects are due on: _____

Differentiated Instruction for World Languages ©2013 Hubbert and Nieminen

Greetings, Responses, and Introductions
Dialogue List

Create Dialogues in the target language
according to target country customs using the following ideas:

- Greet and respond with 5 different people in the class. Include 3 lines per person in the dialogue.

- Greet and ask a store clerk for specific items.

- Call a restaurant/doctor/dentist to make a reservation or appointment.

- Call your Grandma or other relative to ask her to come for dinner.

- Call your teacher or friend about homework that you missed during a sick day.

- You have a new friend with you when going to the movies with a group of friends. Introduce your friend to all.

- Use pictures from a magazine to ask a classmate questions.

- Use pictures from a magazine to help you create a conversation.

- Greet a friend and ask "How are you?" as you meet him/her on the street/at school.

- Your friend is coming to dinner at your house for the first time. Introduce him/her to your parents. Include parents in the dialogue.

- Create a cartoon/comic strip with dialogue.

- After dinner at a friend's house, thank the parents and say goodbye.

- Thank a relative for the birthday present he or she gave you. Tell him/her how much you liked it.

Greetings, Responses, and Introductions Assessment Rubric

Required Content for each dialogue:

- ❖ Correct Grammar
- ❖ Correct Sentence Structure
- ❖ Correct Pronunciation
- ❖ Correct Target Language Vocabulary

Name: _____ Date: _____ Hour: _____

Required elements	Total Points Possible	Points Earned
Grammar	5 points	____ / 5
Sentence Structure	5 points	____ / 5
Pronunciation	5 points	____ / 5
Target Language Vocabulary	5 points	____ / 5
Quality of Presentation	**Total Points Possible**	**Points Earned**
Volume	5 points	____ / 5
Clearly spoken	5 points	____ / 5
Memorized	5 points	____ / 5
Written copy of dialogue to teacher for review/assessment	5 points	____ / 5
TOTAL POINTS POSSIBLE	**40 points**	**TOTAL POINTS EARNED ____ / 40**

Differentiated Instruction for World Languages   ©2013 Hubbert and Nieminen

Colors and Clothing

Select "Three-in-a-Row" to complete the tic-tac-toe.

Create a Scrapbook	Model Your Outfit	Write a Song or a Rap
Create a scrapbook of clothing with different colors using target vocabulary.	Model an outfit you wear to school. As you model, describe your outfit to your audience in the target language.	Write and perform a song or a rap based on the clothing and color vocabulary. 
Create a Matching Game Create a matching game for clothing and colors.	**Your Choice!** 	**Design a PowerPoint** Design a PowerPoint of different clothing in different colors.
Make Paper Dolls Make paper dolls with different outfits. Describe your dolls to the class using target language. 	**Put on a Fashion Show** Put on a fashion show for the class to enjoy. You will need to recruit friends to model five outfits.	**Write a Script** Write a script in the target language for a video that you shoot of people wearing different colors.

- **Challenge 1**: <u>Design and Sew</u> a new outfit. Design, sew, and model a new outfit for the season.
- **Challenge 2**: <u>Design a Magazine</u> for fashion/clothing in the target language.

Design and Sew		Design a Magazine	
* Must be original design	___/ 5	* Appropriate title	___/ 5
* Create rough draft in color	___/ 5	* Min. 20 fully covered pages with illustrations	___/ 5
* Label clothing and colors on design in the target language	___/ 5	* Include short articles	___/ 5
* Give your outfit a name	___/ 5	* Include "ads"	___/ 5
* Sew and model outfit	___/ 5	* Must be in color	___/ 5
Total points	___/ 25	**Total points**	___/ 25

Colors and Clothing Assessment Rubric

Create a Scrapbook		Model Your Outfit		Write a Song or a Rap	
* Min. 5 x 7 in., bound	___/5	* Min. of 6 articles of clothing	___/5	* 1-2 minutes long	___/5
* Min. 20 items of clothing	___/5	* Min. 5 colors included	___/5	* Min. 15 vocabulary terms included	___/5
* Illustrated cover with title and student name	___/5	* Write clothing item names and colors for teacher review	___/5	* Must have melody	___/5
* All items labeled with name and color(s)	___/5	* Use complete sentences when writing and speaking	___/5	* Perform live or play recording	___/5
* Must be in color	___/5	* Present to class	___/5	* Recording or written copy of words to teacher prior to performance for review	___/5
Total points	___/25	Total points	___/25	Total Points	___/25

Create a Matching Game		_____!		Design a PowerPoint	
* 3 x 5 in. index cards	___/5		___/5	* 10 colored content slides	___/5
* Min. 20 cards/10 matches	___/5		___/5	* Title slide with student name	___/5
* Correct spelling and structure required in the target language	___/5		___/5	* Label clothing with colors using correct structure in the target language	___/5
* Use color	___/5		___/5	* Add music to enhance the PowerPoint	___/5
* Include container or carrying bag for cards	___/5		___/5	* Present to class	___/5
Total points	___/25	Total points	___/25	Total points	___/25

Make Paper Dolls		Put on a Fashion Show		Write a Script	
* Make 2 dolls with 3 outfits each	___/5	* Include 5 differently dressed friends	___/5	* Min. 1-2 minutes long	___/5
* Must be in color	___/5	* Write out your outfit descriptions for teacher review/ assessment	___/5	* Min. 10 colors	___/5
* Draw or use magazine/ internet pictures	___/5	* Add music to the show	___/5	* Quality of video and sound	___/5
* Neatness counts	___/5	* Announce show to class with clear pronunciation in the target language	___/5	* Recording/written copy to teacher prior to performance for review	___/5
* Describe your paper dolls to the class	___/5	* Quality of role play (practice is evident)	___/5	* Play video for class	___/5
Total points	___/25	Total points	___/25	Total points	___/25

Show your project choices to your teacher by: _____

All of your projects are due on: _____

Teacher Tips Page for Section C

Standards

Classroom Objects

4.1	3.1/Tech	1.3
1.3		1.1
1.3	1.1	3.1/Math

- **Challenge 1**: 3.1/ELA
- **Challenge 2**: 1.2/ELA

School Subjects, Schedule, and Teachers

1.1	1.3	1.3
1.3		1.1
4.2	3.1/Music	1.3

- **Challenge 1**: 1.3
- **Challenge 2**: 1.1

Family Nouns

1.3	1.3	2.1
1.3		1.3
3.1/Art	1.3	3.2/S.S.

THE ARTS

❖ **Preview Material**
  o For videotaped or recorded products, it is always wise to preview the video or recording prior to class presentation.

❖ **Classroom Objects**
  o Ideas for "Your Choice": Create a horror story about a "classroom object gone crazy", e.g.: a stapler that won't let you stop stapling or a whiteboard that absorbs students and they become animated characters on the board.

❖ **School Subjects, Schedule, and Teachers**
  o Ideas for "Your Choice": Write a story or create a storyboard or a comic about the ideal substitute teacher.

❖ **Family Nouns**
  o Ideas for "Your Choice": Write a song or poem about your family members using target vocabulary; may be factual or fictional.

Classroom Objects

Select two projects to complete.

Create a Game	Organize a PowerPoint	Design a Floor Plan
Create a game with classroom objects using commands.	Organize a PowerPoint with at least 20 classroom objects. 	Illustrate and label your classroom's floor plan in the target language.
Create a Video	Your Choice!	Create an Advertisement
Create a video in the target language by having a friend record you while you are identifying classroom objects.		"Sell" your classroom! Create an advertisement to sell 15 classroom objects using target vocabulary.
Construct a Diorama	Make Flashcards	Create a Graph
Construct your ideal 3-D classroom. What would you include?	Illustrate and label flashcards in the target language with at least 20 classroom objects. 	Count and graph a minimum of 10 different objects; e.g. 25 desks, 3 tables, 2 bookcases, etc.

- **Challenge 1:** Illustrate a Children's Book personifying the classroom objects.
- **Challenge 2:** Create a Booklet that illustrates and labels every possible classroom object. Every object must have one to three sentences that describe the object.

Illustrate a Children's Book		Create a Booklet	
* Min. 5 x 7 in., bound	___ / 5	* Min. 5 x 7 in., bound	___ / 5
* Min. 10 pages	___ / 5	* Min. 10 pages	___ / 5
* Illustrate in color	___ / 5	* Illustrations in color	___ / 5
* Labeled object and/or sentence(s) with each illustration	___ / 5	* Title and author's name on illustrated front cover	___ / 5
* Title and name on front cover, back cover with price, etc.	___ / 5	* Correct spelling and grammar in sentences and labels	___ / 5
Total points	___ / 25	**Total points**	___ / 25

Classroom Objects Assessment Rubric

Create a Game		Organize a PowerPoint		Design a Floor Plan	
* Include 20 commands/objects in the target language	___/5	* Min. 10 content slides	___/5	* Min. 8.5 x 11 in	___/5
* Commands/objects on 3 x 5 in. index cards	___/5	* Title slide with student name	___/5	* Use graph paper	___/5
* Game allows entire class to participate	___/5	* Label each object in target language	___/5	* Classroom objects must be labeled	___/5
* Create simple yet complete rules	___/5	* Must be in color	___/5	* Must be in color	___/5
* Teacher reviews rules prior to play	___/5	* Present to class	___/5	* As close to scale as possible	___/5
Total points	___/25	**Total points**	___/25	**Total Points**	___/25

Create a Video		_____!		Create an Advertisement	
* Include min. 20 objects	___/5		___/5	* Min 8.5 x 11 in.	___/5
* Turn in a written list of objects for teacher review prior to performance	___/5		___/5	* Names of items creatively included	___/5
* Quality of video and sound	___/5		___/5	* Include color picture of each item	___/5
* Clear and correct pronunciation	___/5		___/5	* Create a catchphrase	___/5
* Present the video to class	___/5		___/5	* Price of all items in target country monetary unit	___/5
Total points	___/25	**Total points**	___/25	**Total points**	___/25

Construct a Diorama		Make Flashcards		Create a Graph	
* Min. 1 shoebox size, max. 3 shoeboxes	___/5	* Use 3 x 5 in. index cards	___/5	* Title graph and label axes	___/5
* Min. 20 objects, 5 of which are 3-D	___/5	* 20 objects in color	___/5	* Turn in written summary of conclusions	___/5
* Label all objects in the target language	___/5	* Object on one side, word/phrase on the other	___/5	* Appropriately spaced interval and elements	___/5
* All surfaces decorated	___/5	* Include container or carrying bag for cards	___/5	* Use target language	___/5
* Appropriate title attached to structure	___/5	* Play the game with a partner	___/5	* Display in class	___/5
Total points	___/25	**Total points**	___/25	**Total points**	___/25

Show your project choices to your teacher by: _____

All of your projects are due on: _____

Differentiated Instruction for World Languages   ©2013 Hubbert and Nieminen

School Subjects, Schedule, and Teachers

Select "Three-in-a-Row" to complete the tic-tac-toe.

Write and Perform a Skit	Create an Instruction Card	Take a Survey
Write and perform a skit in the target language with another student asking about each other's schedule.	Make a schedule of subjects, times, and teachers' names for a new student using target vocabulary.	What subjects do your classmates take? Share results in graph format.
Carry out an Interview	**Your Choice!** 	**Tweet**
Interview your teachers; find out some interesting information about them and share your results with your classmates.		Use the 140 character/space limit to tweet about your daily schedule, teachers, and/or favorite subject using the target language.
Research for a Poster	**Write a Song or Rap**	**Construct a 3-D Timeline**
Research a typical school day schedule in the target country. Inform the class of your findings on a poster using the target language.	Write an original song or rap about your favorite subject(s) using the target language.	Construct a 3-D timeline of your school schedule in the target language with subjects and extra-curricular activities.

- **Challenge 1**: Draw a Floor Plan of your school with teachers' names, classroom numbers, subjects, and times for each of your classrooms. Include all other known rooms.
- **Challenge 2:** Create a Questionnaire asking classmates which is their favorite subject and/or class. Share results in written and verbal format.

Draw a Floor Plan		Create a Questionnaire	
* 8.5 x 11 in.	___ / 5	* 8.5 x 11 in., graph must cover at least half of paper	___ / 5
* Use graph paper	___ / 5	* Title graph and label axes	___ / 5
* All objects must be labeled	___ / 5	* Use color	___ / 5
* Must be in color	___ / 5	* Include your original tally sheet	___ / 5
* As close to scale as possible	___ / 5	* Share with and display in class	___ / 5
Total points	___ / 25	**Total points**	___ / 25

School Subjects, Schedule, and Teachers Assessment Rubric

Write and Perform a Skit		Create an Instruction Card		Take a Survey	
* Min. 5 lines per participant	/5	* Max. 5 x 7 in. card	/5	* 8.5 x 11 in., graph must cover at least half of paper	/5
* Correct use of vocabulary terms	/5	* Use heavy paper, cardstock, or index card	/5	* Title graph and label axes in target language	/5
* Script must be turned in for teacher review	/5	* Neatly written or typed	/5	* Use color	/5
* Include props and costumes	/5	* Title your instructions and use numbered steps	/5	* Include your original tally sheet	/5
* Play recording or perform live	/5	* Display in class	/5	* Display in class	/5
Total points	/25	**Total points**	/25	**Total Points**	/25
Carry out an Interview		**_____!**		**Tweet**	
* Min. 5 questions per teacher	/5		/5	* 1-2 Tweets.	/5
* Interview 3-5 teachers	/5		/5	* Use complete sentences	/5
* Q & A written in target language with copy to teacher	/5		/5	* Tweets must be typed in Twitter format	/5
* Include basic bio information	/5		/5	* Use as close to 140 characters as possible	/5
* Share with class	/5		/5	* Use target vocabulary	/5
Total points	/25	**Total points**	/25	**Total points**	/25
Research for a Poster		**Write a Song or Rap**		**Construct a 3-D Timeline**	
* Standard poster size	/5	* 1-2 minutes long	/5	* No larger than 3 ft. long, 1 ft. high	/5
* Illustrations in color (drawings, magazine or internet pictures)	/5	* Min. 6 different lines in target language	/5	* Indicate times of all subjects/classes, breaks and lunch	/5
* Give your poster a title	/5	* Written words to teacher for review/assessment	/5	* Use color	/5
* Schedule included	/5	* Must have melody	/5	* Title your timeline	/5
* Explanation(s) of how schedule reflects the culture of the country	/5	* Perform live or play recording	/5	* Relevant object/picture beside each subject or time	/5
Total points	/25	**Total points**	/25	**Total points**	/25

Show your project choices to your teacher by: _____

All of your projects are due on: _____

Family Nouns

Select "Three-in-a-Row" to complete the tic-tac-toe.

Create a Family Tree	Draw a Family Album	Write a Story
Illustrate and label the tree diagram with blood relatives in the target language. 	Pick ten of your family members, draw and label each in the target language. Describe each with a complete sentence in the target language using at least three adjectives.	Write a story about a family using the target vocabulary of family nouns. Can be factual or fictional. 
Write a News Report Write a news report about your family. Make it exciting! Report it to the class.	Your Choice! 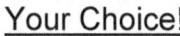	Create a Children's Book Illustrate and label a children's book about family members in the target language.
Paint a Mural Paint a mural. Illustrate and label at least six family members. 	Map it Out Label a map with the locations of your family members.	Construct a Timeline Label each family member's name and year of birth in chronological order using target language. Can be in 3-D. 

Family Nouns Assessment Rubric

Create a Family Tree		Draw a Family Album		Write a Story	
* Min. 14 x 11 in.	___/5	* Min. 5 x 7 in.	___/5	* 2-3 paragraphs	___/5
* Begin with grandparents	___/5	* One family member per page	___/5	* Neatly written or typed	___/5
* Must include color	___/5	* Draw each person in color	___/5	* Use target vocabulary	___/5
* Draw or use real photos of each person	___/5	* Descriptive sentence for each person w/3 adjectives	___/5	* Include beginning, middle, and end	___/5
* Label each person with relationship	___/5	* Present to class	___/5	* Read to class	___/5
Total points	___/25	**Total points**	___/25	**Total Points**	___/25

Write a News Report		_____!		Create a Children's Book	
* Typed, in target language	___/5		___/5	* Min. 5 x 7 in., bound	___/5
* Answer: who, what, when, where, why, and how	___/5		___/5	* Include all family nouns	___/5
* Copy to teacher prior to performance	___/5		___/5	* Illustrations in color for each page	___/5
* Photo/visual with caption	___/5		___/5	* Cover with title and student name	___/5
* Quality of role play (practice is evident)	___/5		___/5	* Correct spelling and grammar	___/5
Total points	___/25	**Total points**	___/25	**Total points**	___/25

Paint a Mural		Map it Out		Construct a Timeline	
* Min. 1 standard poster size, max. size about 4 standard posters	___/5	* Min. 8.5 X 11 in.	___/5	* No larger than 3 ft. long, 1 ft. high	___/5
* Must have a thematic background	___/5	* Min. 7 different locations	___/5	* Use color	___/5
* Title your mural	___/5	* Draw by hand or use actual map	___/5	* Timeline divided into equal yearly units	___/5
* Must be in color	___/5	* Label locations with family noun(s) and name(s) in target language	___/5	* Include 5 important world events during the timeline years	___/5
* Labels must include family noun in target language	___/5	* Include key and compass rose	___/5	* Relevant object/illustration beside each birth date	___/5
Total points	___/25	**Total points**	___/25	**Total points**	___/25

Show your project choices to your teacher by: _____

All of your projects are due on: _____

Unit 2: Connecting with Culture

- ❖ **Teacher Tips for Pages 35 to 42** 34
- ❖ General Heritage and Customs 35
- ❖ Customs and Traditions 37
- ❖ Family Life 39
- ❖ Foods 41
- ❖ **Teacher Tips for Pages 44 to 51** 43
- ❖ Traditional Clothing 44
- ❖ Modern Clothing 46
- ❖ Arts and Education 48
- ❖ Famous People 50

Teacher Tips for Pages 35 to 42

Standards

General Heritage and Customs

4.2	3.2	2.1
2.1	1.3	3.1/Art
2.2/Tech	2.1/Art	1.3

Customs and Traditions

4.2	4.2
2.1	3.2
4.2	3.2
4.2	4.2

Family Life

4.2	2.1	5.1
1.3		1.3
1.3	1.3	3.2

Foods

All Projects			
1.3	2.1	2.2	3.2

➢ **Challenge 1**: 2.2
➢ **Challenge 2**: 2.1

❖ **Preview Material**
  o For videotaped or recorded products, it is always wise to preview the video or recording prior to class presentation.

Familiarize yourself with the Teacher's Choice Project format prior to handing out the *Customs and Traditions* sheet to students.

Teacher's Choice Projects:
  o Excellent group projects.
  o Teacher chooses groups.
  o Teacher assigns project(s) for each group.
  o Teacher gives groups a time limit on presentation.
  o Group presents its project together; all members must be part of presentation.
  o Projects make great displays for the classroom.
  o OPTIONAL: Have each group come up with 2-3 questions about their topic which the teacher then transfers onto a worksheet for students to complete as a quiz.
  o TECHNOLOGY IS FABULOUS: Teachers have students email the questions to them which they then proofread, copy and paste to a document: quiz created. ☺
  o Below is the "**Student Version**" for you to copy or write on the board, if needed.

Teacher's Choice Projects:
  o Teacher chooses groups.
  o Teacher assigns project(s) for each group.
  o Groups have a time limit on presentation: min._____, max. _____ minutes.
  o Group presents project *together;* all members must be part of presentation.
  o Each group creates 2-3 questions about their topic and emails the questions to the teacher.

The General Heritage and Customs of _____.

Complete one from Column I and one more from Columns II or III.

Column I	Column II	Column III
Create a Menu and Write a Recipe Card Create a menu for at least five items and write a detailed recipe card for one dish.	**Identify Characteristics of Family Life** Research the structure and culture of a typical family in the target country. Answer questions such as: Who makes the rules? Is it the parents or grandparents? Identify five characteristics in your speech.	**Write a News Report about the Facts and Figures** Write a news report about the facts and figures of the target language country. Include flag, currency, economy, geography, climate, and government.
Write an Essay on the Education, Language(s), and Religion(s) Write an essay which includes the educational system, languages spoken, and the religions practiced in the target country.	**Create a PowerPoint of the Major Historical Events** Create a PowerPoint of the major historical events of the target language country.	**Create a PowerPoint on Visual and Performing Arts** Create a PowerPoint displaying important visual and performing art/artists in the target country. Can be contemporary.
Create a PowerPoint about Clothing Create a PowerPoint about the traditional and present-day clothing of the target language country.	**Draw a Mural of Jobs and Hobbies** Draw or paint a mural with at least 15 different jobs and hobbies.	**Create a Collage of Customs and Traditions for Different Holidays** Create a collage of the customs and traditions for different holidays.

Differentiated Instruction for World Languages ©2013 Hubbert and Nieminen

General Heritage and Culture Assessment Rubric

Column I | Column II | Column III

Create a Menu and Write a Recipe Card		Identify Characteristics of Family Life		Write a News Report about the Facts and Figures	
* Min. 5 menu items listed	/5	* Min. 5 characteristics	/5	* Min. 2 minutes	/5
* Menu in color with illustrations	/5	* Typed or neatly written	/5	* Min. 3 visual aids	/5
* Neatly written or typed in target language	/5	* Turn in copies of original research material	/5	* Include flag, currency, economy, geography, climate, and government	/5
* Recipe card of authentic ethnic dish in target language	/5	* Typed/written copy to teacher prior to performance for review	/5	* Taped/written script to teacher prior to performance for review	/5
* Correct Spelling	/5	* Present to class	/5	* Play video or perform live	/5
Total points	/25	**Total points**	/25	**Total Points**	/25

Write an Essay: Education, Languages, and Religions		Create a PowerPoint of the Major Historical Events		Create a PowerPoint on Visual and Performing Arts	
* Min. 3 paragraphs	/5	* Min. 10 content slides	/5	* Min. 10 content slides in color	/5
* Must contain all the elements of a well-written essay	/5	* Min. 10 historical events	/5	* Title slide with student name	/5
* Must be typed with copy to teacher	/5	* Title slide with student name	/5	* Min. 10 different works or artists	/5
* Must include resources/bibliography	/5	* Pictures/clip art in color	/5	* Artist info on each slide	/5
* Present to class	/5	* Present to class	/5	* Present to class	/5
Total points	/25	**Total points**	/25	**Total points**	/25

Create a PowerPoint about Clothing		Draw a Mural of Jobs and Hobbies		Create a Collage of Customs and Traditions for Different Holidays	
* Min. 10 content slides	/5	* Min. 24 x 54 in.	/5	* Standard poster size	/5
* Title slide with student name	/5	* Min. 15 illustrations	/5	* Neatly cut pictures from magazines	/5
* Pictures in color with 5 traditional and 5 modern outfits	/5	* Neatly drawn or use magazine/online pictures, all in color	/5	* Min. 5 major holidays	/5
* Brief description of each clothing item/outfit	/5	* Each job/hobby labeled (can be on the reverse side)	/5	* Elements neatly labeled in target language	/5
* Present to class	/5	* Display in classroom	/5	* Present to class	/5
Total points	/25	**Total points**	/25	**Total points**	/25

Show your project choices to your teacher by: _____

All of your projects are due on: _____

Customs and Traditions ~ Teacher's Choice

Gestures for Communication
- Social
- Business
- **Create an Illustrated List** of gestures in the target country

Holidays, Customs and Traditions
- Compare the most important ones with your home country using a **Venn Diagram**
- Choose **One in Detail** and choose your medium

Introductions
- Friends
- Acquaintances
- Business associates
- **Create Dialogues**

Independence Day
- History
- Celebrations
- **Create a Timeline**

Religious Customs
- Births, deaths, weddings, divorces, etc.
- Christenings and baptisms
- Significant religious events of target country
- **Answer Questions** in your choice of medium

School Customs, Dating Customs, and Sports Traditions
- School Customs: Compare yours and the target country's in a **Venn Diagram**
- Dating Customs: Compare yours and the target country's in a **Venn Diagram**
- Sports Traditions: **Create a Comparison Poster**

Customs and Traditions Assessment Rubric

Gestures for Communication~ Illustrated List	
* Min. 5 gestures	____/5
* Illustrations in color	____/5
* Include social and business gestures	____/5
* Neatly written or computer generated	____/5
* Present to class	____/5
Total points	____/ 25

Holidays, Customs, and Traditions Venn Diagram	
* 8.5 x 11 in.	____/5
* Title the diagram and each section	____/5
* Min. 15 holidays, customs, traditions	____/5
* Must be neatly drawn	____/5
* Use color	____/5
Total points	____/ 25

Holidays, Customs, and Traditions ~ One in Detail	
* Name of holiday in target language	____/5
* Illustrations and/or visual aids in color	____/5
* Include foods, decorations, costumes	____/5
* Include when and where, how and why	____/5
* Present in appropriate medium to class	____/5
Total points	____/ 25

Introductions~ Dialogues	
* Create one dialogue for each	____/5
* Min. 6 lines for each dialogue	____/5
* Neatly written or typed	____/5
* Write a paragraph in English explaining the custom of introductions in the target country	____/5
* Present to teacher and/or class	____/5
Total points	____/ 25

Independence Day Timeline	
* No larger than 3 ft. x 1 ft.	____/5
* List 7-10 historical events that led to independence day	____/5
* Dates with descriptions	____/5
* Explain independence-day celebration in one paragraph on a separate sheet	____/5
* Illustration or object in color beside each event/date	____/5
Total points	____/ 25

Religious Customs ~ Answer Questions	
* What impact does religion play in society of target country?	____/5
* Identify major religion(s)	____/5
* What part does religion play in the births, deaths, weddings, etc. in target country?	____/5
* What are the significant religious celebrations/events?	____/5
* The selected medium highlights and enhances topic	____/5
Total points	____/ 25

School or Dating Customs Venn Diagram	
* 8.5 x 11 in.	____/5
* Title the diagram and each section	____/5
* Compare min. 10 elements of yours and target country	____/5
* Must be neatly drawn	____/5
* Use color	____/5
Total points	____/ 25

Sports Traditions Comparison Poster	
* Standard poster size	____/5
* Title the poster	____/5
* Identify each comparison	____/5
* Illustrations in color	____/5
* Label each item by country	____/5
Total points	____/ 25

Show your project choices to your teacher by: _____

All of your projects are due on: _____

Family Life

Select "Three-in-a-Row" to complete the tic-tac-toe.

Compare with a Venn Diagram	Create a Storyboard	Blog about It
Compare families and traditions of the target country with yours. Share your findings with the class verbally.	Create a storyboard about one family tradition in depth from the target country or several in general. 	Find a blog in the target country's language and engage in conversation with a person regarding his/her everyday family life.
Create a Lost Pet Ad	Your Choice!	Create a Photo Album
Create a lost pet ad for your lovable fluff. Think target country pets. Entire ad can be fictional.		Create a photo album about a teenage celebrity and his/her family and pets. Label with names and write a descriptive statement about each member.
Write a Letter	Give a Speech: General and Nonverbal Family Rules and Traditions*	Design a Pets Poster
Pretend you are a person in the target country and you are telling someone about traditions that you have in your family.	Research general and nonverbal family rules and traditions in the target country. Compile your findings into a speech.	Draw and describe typical pets in the target language country.

*For example, in Finland, there is a nonverbal rule that when you walk into someone's house, you remove your shoes.

Family Life Assessment Rubric

Compare with a Venn Diagram		Create a Storyboard		Blog about It	
* Compare min. of 12 items	___/5	* Min. 12 x 18 in.	___/5	* Min. 5 blog entries	___/5
* Name title and sections	___/5	* Min. 6 squares	___/5	* Use target language when possible	___/5
* Neatly drawn	___/5	* Each square requires illustration and explanation of tradition	___/5	* Ask relevant questions using complete sentences	___/5
* Use color to enhance the Venn diagram	___/5	* Neatly written and drawn or computer generated	___/5	* Print out the conversations and turn them in	___/5
* Share with the class	___/5	* Illustrations in color	___/5	* Share your blog entries with the class	___/5
Total points	___/25	**Total points**	___/25	**Total Points**	___/25

Create a Lost Pet Ad		_____!		Create a Photo Album	
* Min. 8.5 x 11 in.	___/5		___/5	* Min. 5x 7 in., bound	___/5
* Describe your pet	___/5		___/5	* Min. 10 pages	___/5
* Illustrate your pet in color	___/5		___/5	* Label each person	___/5
* Must have words "lost pet" in target language	___/5		___/5	* Write a personality description for each person	___/5
* Include contact information	___/5		___/5	* Present to class	___/5
Total points	___/25	**Total points**	___/25	**Total points**	___/25

Write a Letter		Give a Speech: Family Rules and Traditions		Design a Pets Poster	
* Min. 3 paragraphs	___/5	* Min. 2 minutes long	___/5	* Standard poster size	___/5
* Typed, double- spaced, max. size 14 pt. font	___/5	* Min. 2 visual aids	___/5	* Pick top 5-10 pets	___/5
* Proper letter format with correct spelling and grammar	___/5	* Outline to teacher 2 days prior to presentation	___/5	* Describe and label each pet in target language	___/5
* Share typical activities in the lives of a target country family	___/5	* Speak from note cards	___/5	* Give an appropriate title for your poster	___/5
* Read to class	___/5	* Clear voice and pronunciation (practice is evident)	___/5	* Illustrations in color (drawings, magazine or internet pictures)	___/5
Total points	___/25	**Total points**	___/25	**Total points**	___/25

Show your project choices to your teacher by: _____

All of your projects are due on: _____

Foods

Select "Three-in-a-Row" to complete the tic-tac-toe.

Create a Recipe Book	Set the Table	Make a Dish
Create a recipe book for typical foods in the target country. Use one category or several different categories of recipes.	Set a table for four in the manner of the target country. List and illustrate the table setting. Construct a diorama or, if possible, use actual items to showcase to your peers.	Make a typical dish for the target country. Include a recipe and share the dish with your class. 
Plan a Menu	Your Choice! 	Plan a Traditional Party
Plan a menu for one week for a typical family in the target country. Choose your medium.		Plan a traditional party with 6-10 items. Include drinks, appetizers, entrees, desserts, party ware, decorations, etc.
Create a Picture Album	Craft a Collage	Make a Flipbook
Create a picture album with 20 food items. Include pictures and labels for items. 	Craft a collage of different menu items for the target country.	Make a flipbook which includes recipes along with illustrations.

- **Challenge 1:** Using target country staples and spices <u>Create an Original Dish</u> to your liking. Make the dish, include the recipe, and share with the class.
- **Challenge 2:** <u>Write and Illustrate a Complete Menu</u> for a restaurant using target country dishes.

Create an Original Dish		Write and Illustrate a Complete Menu	
* Min. 5 x 7 in. recipe card	___ / 5	* Min. 8.5 x 11 in.	___ / 5
* Include photo or illustration	___ / 5	* Min. 2 pages of menu items with descriptions	___ / 5
*Copy of recipe for teacher prior to presentation	___ / 5	* Illustrated front cover	___ / 5
* Make the dish	___ / 5	* Prices included	___ / 5
* Share dish with class	___ / 5	* Neatly written and drawn or computer generated	___ / 5
Total points	___ / 25	**Total points**	___ / 25

Differentiated Instruction for World Languages ©2013 Hubbert and Nieminen

Foods Assessment Rubric

Create a Recipe Book		Set the Table		Make a Dish	
* Min. 5 x 7 in., bound	/5	* Make diorama or provide actual setting	/5	* Min. 5 x 7 in. recipe card	/5
* Min. 10 recipes	/5	* Make placemats	/5	* Illustration of dish included	/5
* Illustrated cover with title and student name	/5	* Blueprint of table setting for teacher review	/5	* Recipe to teacher for review prior to presentation	/5
* Illustrations in color for each recipe	/5	* Write 5 commands telling someone to set the table	/5	* Share recipe with class	/5
* Neatly written and drawn or computer generated	/5	* Present to class	/5	* Share completed dish with class	/5
Total points	/25	Total points	/25	Total Points	/25

Plan a Menu		____!		Plan a Traditional Party	
* 7 days, 3 meals per day	/5		/5	* Create the menu and plan for the party	/5
* Include times of meals	/5		/5	* State the purpose of the party	/5
* Illustration for each day; min. 1 dish represented	/5		/5	* Describe each item in the plan	/5
* Neatly written and drawn or computer generated	/5		/5	* Illustrate each food item	/5
* Appropriate medium for presentation chosen	/5		/5	* Neatly written and drawn or computer generated	/5
Total points	/25	Total points	/25	Total points	/25

Create a Picture Album		Craft a Collage		Make a Flipbook	
* Min. 5 x 7 in., bound	/5	* Min. 12 x 18 in.	/5	* Min. 8.5 x 11 in., folded	/5
* 20 illustrations in color	/5	* Min. 10 items	/5	* Min. 5 recipes	/5
* Min. 10 pages	/5	* Each menu item labeled in target language (can be on reverse side)	/5	* Include appetizers, entrees, salads, and desserts	/5
* Each food item must be labeled	/5	* Illustrations in color (drawings, magazine or internet pictures)	/5	* Title your flipbook	/5
* Title on front cover, name on back cover	/5	* Title your collage	/5	* Illustrations in color (can be magazine or internet photos)	/5
Total points	/25	Total points	/25	Total points	/25

Show your project choices to your teacher by: _____

All of your projects are due on: _____

Teacher Tips for Pages 44 to 51

Standards

Traditional Clothing

2.1/ELA	2.1/ELA
2.1	2.1/Tech
2.1/Art	2.1

Modern Clothing

2.1	1.3	1.3

➢ Challenge : 1.3

Arts and Education

2.2/Art	1.3	1.3
3.1/L.A.		3.1
1.3	1.3	1.2

➢ Challenge: 1.3/Art

Famous People

3.2	1.3	1.3
1.3	1.3	1.2
1.3	3.2	

❖ **Preview Material**
  o For videotaped or recorded products, it is always wise to preview the video or recording prior to class presentation.
❖ **Traditional Clothing**
  o Review introductions and conclusions with students for speeches and essays prior to project selections.
❖ **Modern Clothing**
  o Prior to projects, have students bring old magazines, clothing catalogues, newspaper ads, and internet pictures portraying target country fashions. The projects are enhanced by visiting the computer lab so that students can see authentic and current fashions.
❖ **Arts and Education:** Example of an Education Recipe Card:

Recipe for Finland's Educational System	
1 cup of excellent teacher salaries	A heaping helping of no organized school sports
5 tbsp. of quality teachers	4 barrels of quality, hot food every school day
15 tsp. of recess every hour	2 cups of the same books, same lesson strategies and timelines throughout the country

Use these ingredients as follows:
1. Entrance to university and teacher training is based on talent, not on whether you have the money for college. Schooling is free, but exams for admittance are vigorous.
2. Studies have shown that taking a long enough break often enough improves one's ability to learn and retain information. In Finland, students go outside, rain or shine, for 15 minutes every hour.
3. Sports and recreation are separate from the school environment. No money or time is spent from the school budget on organized sports.
4. School books, supplies, and quality, warm food are all provided to everyone free of charge.
5. Quality food is served: homemade-style casseroles, soup, salads, etc. No hamburgers, hot dogs, or fast food-type fare is served.
6. When/if you have to move during a school year, you will fit right in.

❖ **Famous People**
  o Ideas for "Your Choice": Make a collage of famous people, and then cut it into puzzle pieces for friends to put together. Follow a famous person on Twitter or Facebook for a week, and then write a summary about his/her activities. Write an obituary for a living celebrity.

 # Traditional Clothing and Costumes

To accomplish this project, you will need to complete two assignments.

1. Choose either a speech *or* an essay.
2. Choose a visual presentation of the traditional clothing and costumes.
3. Show your project choices to your teacher by: _____.
4. All of your projects are due on: _____.

Each province/state/area in the target country has a different costume. Select either a speech to give *or* an essay to write. Your task is to answer the following questions:

- ❖ Why do the countries have different costumes?
- ❖ When are they worn?
- ❖ What do the colors signify?
- ❖ Who wears the costumes?
- ❖ What is the symbolism for the costumes?
- ❖ Where are the costumes worn? (For what occasion(s) are they worn?)

After choosing a speech or an essay, pick *one* of the other four choices below for the visual presentation of the traditional clothing and costumes:

- ❖ <u>Create a Photo-folio.</u> Create a photo-folio of all the target country's traditional clothing. Include names of costumes and locations.
- ❖ <u>Generate a PowerPoint.</u> Pick an area (e.g. north, south, west, or east) and create a PowerPoint of the traditional costumes.
- ❖ <u>Make Paper Dolls.</u> Provide a detailed description of one particular costume of the target country. Include the man's and woman's costumes.
- ❖ <u>Design a Poster.</u> Pick an area (e.g. north, south, west, or east) and provide a detailed description of five costumes in that area. Include the men's and women's costumes; draw and label each.

Traditional Clothing and Costumes Assessment Rubric

Choose one:

Give a Speech		Write an Essay	
* Min. 2 minutes long	___/5	* Min. 250 words	___/5
* All questions clearly answered	___/5	* All questions clearly answered	___/5
* Copy of speech to teacher for review prior to performance	___/5	* Typed with correct essay format	___/5
* Use notecards for presentation	___/5	* Include sources used	___/5
* Sufficient volume and clear pronunciation	___/5	* Correct spelling and grammar required	___/5
Total points	___/25	**Total Points**	___/25

Choose one:

Create a Photo-folio		Generate a PowerPoint	
* Min. 5 x 7 in., bound	___/5	* Min. 10 slides of traditional costumes	___/5
* Min. 10 costumes	___/5	* Each slide includes appropriate photo(s) and label(s)	___/5
*Costumes appropriately labeled	___/5	* Must be in color	___/5
* Must be in color	___/5	* Background must support and enhance content	___/5
* Cover page with title and student name	___/5	* Title slide with appropriate title and student name	___/5
Total points	___/25	**Total points**	___/25

Make Paper Dolls		Design a Poster	
* Min. 1 detailed costume per gender	___/5	* Standard poster size	___/5
* Use cardstock or heavy paper	___/5	* Min. 5 costumes	___/5
* Must be in color	___/5	* Appropriately titled	___/5
* Create a display stand	___/5	* Must be in color	___/5
* Label name of costume and location on display stand	___/5	* Label costumes with locations	___/5
Total points	___/25	**Total points**	___/25

Differentiated Instruction for World Languages ©2013 Hubbert and Nieminen

Modern Clothing

Students use clothing vocabulary in real life situations. For this project, students should research the target country's clothing customs. Through this project, students will realize that clothing is an important form of expression in all cultures.

	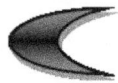	
1-3 person group	1-3 person group	1-3 person group
Create a Dialogue in the target language with a clothing store clerk or a friend discussing clothing items at a particular store. ☐Write out the dialogue and include a description of the location.	Describe your School's Dress Code in the target language. You may come up with a "new" dress code if you wish. You will need to present your rules to the "school board" or "the principal"; i.e. your teacher and class.	Create a Mini Catalog of modern fashions using the target language. The prices must be in the target country's currency. Present to class. You will need to describe and give details of the choices of fashion items that you included in the catalog.

All clothing choices must be school appropriate.

> **Challenge**: Be the Designer and put on a fashion show.

Be the Designer	
* Five outfits	____/5
* Written description for each outfit	____/5
* Brief bio of designer	____/5
* Music must be included	____/5
* Present to class (recruit friends as models)	____/5
Total points	____/ 25

Modern Clothing Assessment Rubric

⚡		🌙		⭐	
* Include min. 3 clothing items	___/5	* Min. 10 rules	___/5	* Min. 5 x 7 in.	___/5
* Min. 15 lines	___/5	* Create "guidelines" poster	___/5	* Min. 15 items	___/5
* Min. 1 visual aid/prop for each clothing item	___/5	* Neatly written or typed information	___/5	* Each illustration/picture must have a description of clothing item with price	___/5
* Neatly written or typed	___/5	* Each "rule" must have an illustrated example	___/5	* All illustrations in color (drawings, magazine or internet pictures)	___/5
* Each member of the group must present	___/5	* Each member of the group must present	___/5	* Each member of the group must present	___/5
Total points	___/ 25	**Total points**	___/ 25	**Total Points**	___/ 25

Show your project choices to your teacher by: _____

All of your projects are due on: _____

Arts and Education

Select "Three-in-a-Row" to complete the tic-tac-toe.

Draw a Portrait of an Artist	Create a Diorama	Write a Recipe Card
Research a famous visual artist. Write a paragraph describing the artist and his work. Draw a portrait of the artist.	Take an online tour of a museum in the target country. Create a diorama of the museum with historical and/or contemporary works of art.*	Write a "recipe card" for the educational system of the target country. 
Design a Book Cover or a Poster	Your Choice!	Perform Live on Stage
Create a book cover or a poster of important and/or popular literary works of the target country.		Research a composer/ performer and write a speech about the person or give a performance of a work he/she has done.
Create a Brochure	Create a Bio	Write a Letter
Create a brochure describing different types of schools in the target language country.	Create a short bio and a description of the work of a choreographer or performance artist from the target language country.	Write a letter to an artist or an educator inquiring about his/ her profession. 

*Other suggestions for the diorama: musical instruments, painting, sculpture, handiworks, cultural museum.

> **Challenge:** Reproduce Art or a Building. Reproduce an important piece of art from the target country or an important building in the target country. If the original art is 3-D, you must reproduce in 3-D, if 2-D, then 2-D, etc. Building may be drawn.

Reproduce Art or a Building	
* Min. 8.5 x 11 in. for 2-D, min. 5 in. height for 3-D	____/5
* Include a picture of original art or building	____/5
* In original color	____/5
* Bio of artist or architect	____/5
* Quality effort	____/5
Total points	____/25

Arts and Education Assessment Rubric

Draw a Portrait of an Artist		Create a Diorama		Write a Recipe Card	
* Min. 8.5 x 11 in. portrait size	/5	* Approx. 10 x 32 x 28 in. or two standard shoe boxes	/5	* Min. 5 x 7 in. card	/5
* Separate sheet for bio and work information of artist	/5	* Min. 10 art pieces	/5	* Min. 5 "ingredients"	/5
* Info neatly written or typed	/5	* Must be in color	/5	* Neatly written or typed	/5
* Draw the portrait using medium of your choice	/5	* All surfaces must be decorated	/5	* Illustration in color	/5
* Present to class	/5	* Name of museum and country on the title card	/5	* Numbered steps for recipe "completion"	/5
Total points	/ 25	**Total points**	/ 25	**Total Points**	/ 25
Design a Book Cover or a Poster		_____!		Perform Live on Stage	
* Book cover 8.5 x 11 in., poster standard size	/5		/5	* 1-2 minutes long	/5
* Min. 5 literary works	/5		/5	* Typed bio of composer/performer	/5
* Title of work and author must be included for each work	/5		/5	* Written or typed outline of speech or performance to teacher for review prior to presentation	/5
* Brief description of each work	/5	*	/5	* Quality of performance (practice is evident)	/5
* Must be in color	/5		/5	* Present to class	/5
Total points	/ 25	**Total points**	/ 25	**Total points**	/ 25
Create a Brochure		Create a Bio		Write a Letter	
* 8.5 x 11 in., folded	/5	* Neatly written or typed	/5	* Must be typed	/5
* Neatly written and drawn or computer generated	/5	* Name of artist as title	/5	* Ask a min. of 5 questions	/5
* Min. 3 types of schools	/5	* Bio must have min. 5 pieces of factual information	/5	* Must be in correct letter format	/5
* Illustrations in color	/5	* Description must be in complete sentences	/5	* Copy of letter and addressed envelope to teacher prior to mailing	/5
* Title on front cover, name on back cover	/5	* Include sources	/5	* Min. 1 paragraph if target language, 3 if in English	/5
Total points	/ 25	**Total points**	/ 25	**Total points**	/ 25

Show your project choices to your teacher by: _____

All of your projects are due on: _____

Famous People

Select one to complete.

Draw and Color a Picture
Draw and color a picture of a famous person in the target country.

Who is it? Poster
Create a poster of a famous person. Include name, DOB, living/dead, famous for, etc. Make it creative.

Craft a 3-D Timeline
Craft a 3-D timeline of your chosen person's life.

Design a Scrapbook
Design a scrapbook of a famous person's life who is still alive. Include copies of photos of the person.

Make a Collage
Make a collage about the famous person and discuss the person's major accomplishments.

"Interview" a Famous Person
"Interview" your famous person of choice. You need to create questions to ask with answers, and then get a partner to ask the questions while you play the famous person.

You Be the Person
Act out a dialogue or monologue of the famous person you have chosen to be. Discuss major accomplishments of the person.

Create a PowerPoint
Create an interactive PowerPoint for the class about a famous person from the target country.

Your Choice!

Famous People Assessment Rubric

Draw and Color a Picture		Who is it? Poster		Craft a 3-D Timeline	
* Min. 8.5 x 11 in.	/5	* Standard poster size	/5	* No larger than 3 ft. long, 1 ft. high	/5
* Neatly written sentences, drawing in color	/5	* Neatly written or typed info	/5	* Min. 15 events	/5
* Brief bio of person with at least one sentence description	/5	* Title must include name of person	/5	* Description of each event with date included	/5
* Include reason why the person is famous in the bio	/5	* Illustration(s) in color	/5	* Relevant object/illustration in 3-D form beside each event	/5
* Present to or display in class	/5	* All info in target language	/5	* Use color	/5
Total points	/ 25	**Total points**	/ 25	**Total Points**	/ 25
Design a Scrapbook		**Make a Collage**		**"Interview" a Famous Person**	
* Min. 5 x7 in., bound	/5	* Standard poster size	/5	* 10 questions and answers	/5
* Min. 10 pages	/5	* Min. 25 pictures	/5	* Neatly written or typed Q & A for teacher review	/5
* Neatly written or typed sentence for each page	/5	* Labeled (can be on reverse side)	/5	* Create a meaningful prop or costume for interview	/5
* Illustrations in color	/5	* Appropriate title	/5	* Must be in target language	/5
* Title on front cover, name on back cover	/5	* Use color to enhance your collage	/5	* Present to class	/5
Total points	/ 25	**Total points**	/ 25	**Total points**	/ 25
You Be The Person		**Create a PowerPoint**		_____!	
* Min. 15 lines	/5	* Min. 10 content slides	/5		/5
* Typewritten script for teacher review	/5	* Meaningful title	/5		/5
* Discuss major accomplishments	/5	* Graphics in color	/5		/5
* Create a meaningful prop or costume for presentation	/5	* Grammatically and structurally correct	/5		/5
* Present to class	/5	* Delivered as an interactive presentation	/5		/5
Total points	/ 25	**Total points**	/ 25	**Total points**	/ 25

Show your project choices to your teacher by: _____

All of your projects are due on: _____

Differentiated Instruction for World Languages ©2013 Hubbert and Nieminen

Unit 3: Home and Abroad

- ❖ Teacher Tips Page for Unit 3 53
- ❖ House and Home 54
- ❖ Neighborhood and Directions 56
- ❖ City and Transportation 58

Teacher Tips Page for Unit 3

Standards

House and Home		
1.1	3.2/Art	1.3
2.2		3.1/Art
1.3	3.2	1.3

House and Home
Conversations with Family

All dialogues		
1.1	1.2	1.3

Neighborhood and Directions		
4.1	1.3	1.3
1.3		1.3
1.3/Math	3.1/S.S.	1.1

City and Transportation		
2.2	1.3	4.2
1.3		4.2/Tech
1.3	4.1	1.3

- ❖ **Preview Material**
    - o For videotaped or recorded products, it is always wise to preview the video or recording prior to class presentation.
- ❖ **House and Home**
    - o Use rubric on page 23 to assess dialogues, if needed.
- ❖ **Neighborhood and Directions:** Amazing Race Scavenger Hunt
    - o This activity can be a group activity; the students make up the directions and create the "treasure" to be found. It can also be played in an "orienteering" fashion; the students get a stamp on their "passports" as they find the correct location through the directions given.
- ❖ **City and Transportation**
    - ➤ **Challenge:** Create a Map Game. Create a map game of the capital city, a target country, or a section/region of the target country. Include destination places for tourists to visit and directions on how to get to the destinations. **Challenge**: 3.1/S.S.

Create a Map Game	
* Min. 12 x 18 in. in size	____/5
* Min. 5 destinations	____/5
* Include directional vocabulary on game activity cards	____/5
* Must be in target language	____/5
* State the significance of the destination on game board spaces	____/5
Total points	___/ 25

House and Home

Select two projects to complete.

Describe Your Room	Be an Architect	Create a Matching Activity Worksheet
Describe your room in detail using target vocabulary.	Draw a typical house in the target country. 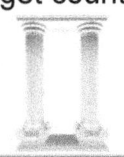	Create a matching activity of appliances and tableware.
Create a List	**Your Choice!**	**Craft a Diorama**
Create a list of objects using the category: Outside Elements and Objects. (E.g. garage, mower, fence, garden, trees, etc.)		Craft a diorama of your dream room using target vocabulary.
Draw a Floor Plan	**Write a Journal**	**Describe and Draw**
Draw a floor plan of your bedroom or another room in your house and label it using target vocabulary.	Write about daily chores you might need to accomplish while living in a target country family. 	Describe furniture in your dream house. Then have someone else draw it as you describe it aloud. This is a partner activity; both must complete all assessment steps.

Students create a dialogue or have a conversation based on the following topics:
- May I borrow the car?
- May I have money for new shoes/jeans/movie/a phone?
- What do you want for your birthday/Christmas/graduation?
- What do you talk about around the dinner table?
- Ask a grandparent about childhood/job/favorite things.

Required Content for each dialogue:
- Correct Grammar
- Correct Sentence Structure
- Correct Pronunciation
- Correct Vocabulary Used

House and Home Assessment Rubric

Describe Your Room		Be an Architect		Create a Matching Activity Worksheet	
* Min. 10 items in room	/5	* Min. 8.5 x 11 in.	/5	* Min. 8.5 x 11 in.	/5
* Neatly written or typed	/5	* Include surrounding elements	/5	* Illustrations in color	/5
* Use complete sentences	/5	* In color	/5	* Use target language	/5
* 2-3 adjectives per item description	/5	* 5 specific details labeled in target language	/5	* Min. 10 item illustrations on left side	/5
* Draw a picture of the room in color	/5	* Brief explanation of characteristics of typical house on separate sheet	/5	* Matching item names in random order on the right side	/5
Total points	/ 25	Total points	/ 25	Total Points	/ 25

Create a List		_____!		Craft a Diorama	
* 8.5 x 11 in.	/5		/5	* Min. 1 shoebox size (or approx. 5x14x16)	/5
* Min. 20 items	/5		/5	* Min. 10 labeled items in target language	/5
* Neatly written or computer generated in target language	/5		/5	* Min. three 3-D objects	/5
* Illustrate a min. of 10 items	/5		/5	* All surfaces must be decorated	/5
* Title your list appropriately	/5		/5	* Title your diorama	/5
Total points	/ 25	Total points	/ 25	Total points	/ 25

Draw a Floor Plan		Write a Journal		Describe and Draw	
* Min. 12 x 18 in.	/5	* Neatly written or typed	/5	* Type description	/5
* Min. 15 items; remember doors and windows	/5	* Include 10 chores	/5	* Describe 5 items in target language	/5
* Draw objects or use magazine/online pictures	/5	* Each entry must have dates and days of week	/5	* Use a min. of 5 descriptive terms (color, shape, size, etc.)	/5
* Must be as close to scale as possible	/5	* Record at least one chore per day	/5	* Drawing must be in color	/5
* Present to class	/5	* Written in 1st person in target language	/5	* Turn in drawing; must be signed by student artist	/5
Total points	/ 25	Total points	/ 25	Total points	/ 25

Show your project choices to your teacher by: _____

All of your projects are due on: _____

Neighborhood and Directions

Select "Three-in-a-Row" to complete the tic-tac-toe.

Draw a Map	Make a List and Draw	Amazing Race Scavenger Hunt
Draw a map of your neighborhood. Label 12 destinations and/or streets on the map. 	Draw a floor plan of the inside of the school and make a list of directions that take the reader around the school.	Record/Write instructions for classmates to follow to find token treasures! This is a great partner activity. 
Create a Game	Your Choice! 	Draw and Label a Map
Create a game with directions to destinations on the game board. Include directions on how to play.		Draw and label a map from your house to the school or other known destination. Include directions to and from. Use target language.
Survey and Graph	Draw a Neighborhood Map	Play Blind Man's Bluff
Survey your classmates: How far do they live from the school or your house? Map and graph the results. 	Pick a neighborhood (or choose the city center) in the target language country; copy and label the map with a minimum of 12 streets and locations/buildings/businesses.	Give detailed instructions to classmates so they can find their way around the classroom while blindfolded. 

Differentiated Instruction for World Languages ©2013 Hubbert and Nieminen

Neighborhood and Directions Assessment Rubric

Draw a Map		Make a List and Draw		Amazing Race Scavenger Hunt	
* 8.5 x 11 in.	/5	* 8.5 x 11 in.	/5	* Min. 10 instructions	/5
* Labels and streets in target language	/5	* Include 8 directions in the target language	/5	* Clearly written and/or spoken directions in target language	/5
* In color	/5	* Drawn to scale	/5	* Create a token for each location players will visit	/5
* Include compass rose and key	/5	* Label each room (e.g. office, gym, etc.) in the target language	/5	* Create a "loot bag" for each player	/5
* As close to scale as possible	/5	* Use color to enhance your floor plan	/5	* Creative tokens	/5
Total points	/25	**Total points**	/25	**Total Points**	/25

Create a Game		_____!		Draw and Label a Map	
* Min. 11 x 17 in.	/5		/5	* 12 x 18 in.	/5
* Min. 15 directions/ instruction cards in the target language	/5		/5	* Label destination and departure point	/5
* 4 themed game pieces and appropriate title	/5		/5	* Label 5 other locations on the way	/5
* In color	/5		/5	* Directions to and from in target language	/5
* Complete set of rules and directions	/5		/5	* As close to scale as possible	/5
Total points	/25	**Total points**	/25	**Total points**	/25

Survey and Graph		Draw a Neighborhood Map		Play Blind Man's Bluff	
* Map and graph on separate sheets	/5	* 12 x 18 in.	/5	* Instructions written on 3 x 5 in. index cards	/5
* 8.5 x 11 in. each sheet	/5	* 12 locations labeled in target language	/5	* Min. 5 different destinations	/5
* Survey min. 10 classmates in the target language	/5	* City must be from target country	/5	* Min. 10 directions in target language	/5
* Use color in the graph	/5	* In color	/5	* Clearly spoken instructions	/5
* Label the map with classmate names	/5	* Include compass rose and key	/5	* Be the instructor; lead the game	/5
Total points	/25	**Total points**	/25	**Total points**	/25

Show your project choices to your teacher by: _____

All of your projects are due on: _____

City and Transportation

Select "Three-in-a-Row" to complete the tic-tac-toe.

Draw a Cityscape	Create a Travel Brochure	Compare with a Venn Diagram
Draw a cityscape of a city in the target country. 	Create a travel brochure for the capital city of the target country. Include five tourist destinations in the city. Use target language.	Compare city transportation in your city/town and city/town of equal size in the target country.
Create Instructions	Your Choice!	Create a PowerPoint
Create instructions on how to get around the capital city in the target country; pick a destination to go to from the airport, central bus, or train station.		Pick ten tourist destinations in the target country. Create a PowerPoint presentation and be ready to share.
Design a Postcard	Be a Travel Guide	Illustrate a Poster
Design three postcards to send to your family from a city or cities in the target country.	Pretend you are a travel guide on a bus trip. Videotape yourself telling all the tourists what they are looking at as you travel through a city in the target country.	Illustrate a poster sharing the major forms of transportation in the target country. 

City and Transportation Assessment Rubric

Draw a Cityscape		Create a Travel Brochure		Compare with a Venn Diagram	
* 12 x 18 in.	/5	* 8.5 x 11 in., folded	/5	* 8.5 x 11 in.	/5
* Must be length of paper	/5	* Neatly written and drawn or computer generated	/5	* Title diagram and label sections	/5
* Background silhouette must be hand drawn	/5	* 5 destinations included	/5	* Min. 15 comparison items	/5
* Foreground may use magazine cut-outs, must be in color	/5	* Title fold must have illustration	/5	* Must be in color	/5
* Title must include city and country names	/5	* Must be in color	/5	* Neatly drawn	/5
Total points	/25	**Total points**	/25	**Total Points**	/25

Create Instructions		_____!		Create a PowerPoint	
* 8.5 x 11 in.	/5		/5	* Min. 10 content slides	/5
* Typed instructions in target language	/5		/5	* Title slide name	/5
* Draw a map that contains at least the main roads	/5		/5	* Photo(s) and label(s) on each slide	/5
* Map must be in color	/5		/5	* Seamless slide transitions	/5
* Clearly label departure point and destination	/5		/5	* Clear pronunciation and adequate volume during presentation	/5
Total points	/25	**Total points**	/25	**Total points**	/25

Design a Postcard		Be a Travel Guide		Illustrate a Poster	
* 4 x 6 in. cardstock or heavy paper	/5	* 2-3 minutes long with correct pronunciation	/5	* Standard poster size	/5
* Color illustration must be a significant location in target country and labeled	/5	* Create appropriate props/background	/5	* Label each form of transportation in target language	/5
* Write message in target language	/5	* Written monologue in target language for teacher review	/5	* Illustrations in color (drawings, magazine or internet pictures)	/5
* Address the card	/5	* Include min. 8 city sights	/5	* Title the poster	/5
* Create a postage stamp	/5	* Present video to class	/5	* Include percentage of population usage for each	/5
Total points	/25	**Total points**	/25	**Total points**	/25

Show your project choices to your teacher by: _____

All of your projects are due on: _____

Unit 4: Body and Mind

- ❖ Teacher Tips Page for Unit 4 61
- ❖ Parts of the Body 62
- ❖ Sports and Hobbies 64
- ❖ Feelings and Emotions 66
- ❖ Technology 68

Teacher Tips Page for Unit 4

Standards

Parts of the Body

1.3	1.3
3.1/Art	1.2
1.3	1.3

Feelings and Emotions

1.1	1.1
1.1	4.1
1.1	1.1
1.3	1.1
3.1/ELA	1.1

Sports and Hobbies

1.3	3.1/Math	1.3
1.2		1.3
1.3	1.3	3.2

➢ **Challenge 1**: 3.2/Tech
➢ **Challenge 2**: 3.2/Music

Technology

5.1	3.1/Tech
3.1/Tech	1.3
2.2	2.2
1.3	1.3

❖ **Preview Material**
  o For videotaped or recorded products, it is always wise to preview the video or recording prior to class presentation.

❖ **Parts of the Body**
  Examples of goofy remedies:
  o Tennis elbow~ Apply cornbread mixture and bake 30 minutes @ 250F.
  o Sore throat~ Hang upside down from the rafters for 15 minutes twice daily.
  o Stomach ache~ Perform 3 somersaults immediately after a meal of chili dogs.

❖ **Feelings and Emotions**
  o For "Use Vocabulary in a Sentence," have students illustrate each of the sentences for extra credit.

❖ **Sports and Hobbies**
  o Ideas for Your Choice: Be a Sports Announcer. Create a monologue with a minimum of 10 sentences using target vocabulary.

❖ **Technology**
  o Make a copy of the Facebook template on page 110-111 to show students and to familiarize yourself with the format.

Parts of the Body

Choose one project to complete.

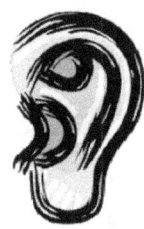

Make a poster

Make a poster with labeled pictures of target vocabulary.

Draw a Self-Portrait

Draw a self-portrait and label parts of the body using target vocabulary.

Create a 3-D Mr. or Mrs. Potato Head

Create a 3-D Mr. or Mrs. Potato Head using a potato/clay and other household or craft items.

Perform a Skit

You are the doctor: patients complain about different parts of the body. Prescribe goofy remedies.

Cut Out Photos of Celebrities

Cut out photos of celebrities from magazines; label the parts of their bodies.

Create a New Person

Cut out 12 different parts of the body from magazines to create a new person!

Parts of the Body Assessment Rubric

Make a Poster		Draw a Self-Portrait	
* Standard poster size	___/5	* Min. 8.5 x 11 in	___/5
* Include all target vocabulary	___/5	* Label using target vocabulary	___/5
* Illustrations in color	___/5	* Draw in color	___/5
* Each illustration clearly labeled	___/5	* Title your drawing	___/5
* Title your poster	___/5	* Display in or share with class	___/5
Total points	___/ 25	**Total points**	___/ 25

Create a 3-D Mr. or Mrs. Potato Head		Perform a Skit	
* Min. 5 in. high	___/5	* "Visit" with a min. of 3 "patients"	___/5
* Use a real potato or clay for the body	___/5	* Neatly written or typed; script for teacher review prior to performance	___/5
* Make body parts and accessories like those of Mr./Mrs. Potato Head	___/5	* Correct target vocabulary	___/5
* 2 sets of parts and accessories	___/5	* Goofy remedies included	___/5
* Sketch your potato people and label the body parts in the target language	___/5	* Perform to class	___/5
Total points	___/ 25	**Total points**	___/ 25

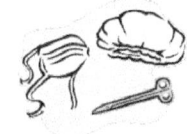

Cut Out Photos of Celebrities		Create a New Person	
* 12 x 18 in.	___/5	* Min. 8.5 x 11 in	___/5
* Min. 5 photos	___/5	* Label all parts using target vocabulary	___/5
* Min. 5 parts per photo labeled	___/5	* Brief bio of new person	___/5
* Use all target vocabulary	___/5	* Give the person a new name as headline for work	___/5
* Include celebrity names and title your work	___/5	* Your name on the back	___/5
Total points	___/ 25	**Total points**	___/ 25

Differentiated Instruction for World Languages ©2013 Hubbert and Nieminen

Sports and Hobbies

Select two projects to complete.

Create a Commercial	Conduct a Survey	Create a Booklet
Create a commercial for the upcoming season for your favorite sports team or hobby.	Survey your classmates in the target language to find out their favorite sports and/or hobbies. Create a graph based on your results.	Create a booklet with illustrations on how to play a particular sport or "how-to" for a hobby.
Create a Dictionary	Your Choice!	Design a Game
Create a dictionary in alphabetical order for a sport or hobby in the target language. 		Design a game using either your favorite sport or hobby. 
Create Trading Cards	Give a Speech	Create a Bio
Create a set of trading cards for your favorite sports figures or important people in a hobby of your choice.	Give a speech as you accept an MVP award for your chosen sport or a trophy for your hobby.	Create a bio about a sports celebrity in the target country with a photo and bio information.

- **Challenge 1:** <u>Create an Instructional Video</u> on how to play a sport or how to do your hobby.
- **Challenge 2:** <u>Create an Original Theme Song</u> for your favorite sports team or hobby.

Create an Instructional Video		**Write a Theme Song**	
* 2-3 minutes long	/5	* Min. 6 original lines in target language	/5
* Must be in target language	/5	* Must include name of team or hobby	/5
* Clear pronunciation and adequate volume	/5	* Must have melody	/5
* Copy of video to teacher for review prior to performance	/5	* Copy of words or recording to teacher for review prior to performance	/5
* Share video with class	/5	* Perform live or play recording	/5
Total points	/25	**Total points**	/25

Differentiated Instruction for World Languages ©2013 Hubbert and Nieminen

Sports and Hobbies Assessment Rubric

Create a Commercial		Conduct a Survey		Create a Booklet	
* Min. 1 minute long	____/5	* Survey min. 10 people	____/5	* 5 x 7 in., bound	____/5
* Min. 2 visual aids	____/5	* Appropriate title	____/5	* Neatly written and drawn or computer generated	____/5
* Include expression in target language	____/5	* Label axes	____/5	* Instructions clearly written in target language	____/5
* Script to teacher for review prior to performance	____/5	* Appropriate interval for elements	____/5	* Include illustrations	____/5
* Perform live or play video	____/5	* Must use color in graph	____/5	* Cover must have title and student name	____/5
Total points	____/25	**Total points**	____/25	**Total Points**	____/25

Create a Dictionary		_____!		Design a Game	
* Min. 5 x 7 in., bound	____/5		____/5	* Min. 20 question/activity cards in the target language	____/5
* Min. 20 vocabulary words defined	____/5		____/5	* Thematic title	____/5
* Illustrations in color (drawings, magazine or internet pictures)	____/5		____/5	* Set of rules	____/5
* Alphabetical order	____/5		____/5	* Devise a plan on how the game is played	____/5
* Include title and student name on the cover	____/5		____/5	* Lead the game	____/5
Total points	____/25	**Total points**	____/25	**Total points**	____/25

Create Trading Cards		Give a Speech		Create a Bio	
* 3 x 5 in. index cards	____/5	* Min. 1 minute long	____/5	* 12 x 18 in. poster	____/5
* Make at least 10 cards, use target language	____/5	* Script to teacher for review prior to speech	____/5	* Include color photo or illustration	____/5
* Include names and stats of athletes/hobbyists	____/5	* Create the award/trophy	____/5	* Use target language only	____/5
* Illustration(s) in color (drawings, magazine or internet pictures)	____/5	* Delivered with appropriate volume and excitement in the target language	____/5	* Bio must be factual	____/5
* Your name in lower left-hand corner on each card	____/5	* Quality of presentation (practice is evident)	____/5	* Present to class	____/5
Total points	____/25	**Total points**	____/25	**Total points**	____/25

Show your project choices to your teacher by: _____

All of your projects are due on: _____

Differentiated Instruction for World Languages ©2013 Hubbert and Nieminen

Feelings and Emotions
Choose two projects from the list to complete.

Use Feelings-and-Emotions Vocabulary in a Sentence
For example: We are_____ (happy). I am _____ (healthy).

Create a Poster
Illustrate and label feelings/emotions vocabulary on a poster. You may use magazine or internet pictures.

Create a Children's Book
Create a children's book with illustrations about feelings and emotions.

Make a List of Antonyms
List English antonym pairs (e.g. sad/happy) and then find the translations in target language.

Design Flip Books
Design 3 flip books with pictures on the front and target language feelings/emotions vocabulary on the inside flap.

Create Greeting Cards
Create the following greeting cards: 1. Birthday for a boy, 2. Birthday for a girl, 3. Sympathy, 4. Thank you, and 5. Congratulations. Use the target language.

Create a Video for "Drama 101"
Videotape teachers or friends talking about feelings and emotions; have each person act out two emotions or feelings. Narrate with a sentence in the target language describing their performances.

Create a Collage Quiz
Create a collage quiz to showcase different feelings and emotions. Pictures on one side, target vocabulary on the other side.

Write a Story
Write a story using target emotions/feelings vocabulary.

Write a Diary or Journal Entry
Monitor your emotions and feelings for one week. For each day, write out at least two sentences describing your well-being.

Feelings and Emotions Assessment Rubric

Use Vocabulary in a Sentence		Create a Poster	
* 15-20 sentences	/5	* Standard poster size	/5
* Use different subjects	/5	* Min. 20 illustrations	/5
* Must be complete sentences	/5	* Illustrate in color	/5
* Neatly written or typed	/5	* Label pictures in target language	/5
* Correct spelling and grammar	/5	* Title your poster	/5
Total points	/25	**Total points**	/25

Create a Children's Book		Make a List of Antonyms	
* Min. 5 x 7 in.	/5	* Min. 15 antonym pairs	/5
* Min. 10 pages	/5	* Use 5 pairs in sentences	/5
* Min. 10 target vocabulary expressions	/5	* Correct structure	/5
* Illustrations in color	/5	* Illustrate 5 of the antonym pairs	/5
* Cover page with title and name	/5	* Neatly written or typed	/5
Total points	/25	**Total points**	/25

Design Flip Books		Create Greeting Cards	
* Each book 8.5 x 11 in., folded	/5	* Min. 5 x 7 in.	/5
* 5 emotions per book	/5	* Message with target vocabulary	/5
* Illustrations in color	/5	* Neatly written or computer generated	/5
* Descriptive sentence inside for each word	/5	* Illustrations in color	/5
* Underline target word	/5	* Trademark and name on back	/5
Total points	/25	**Total points**	/25

Create a Video for "Drama 101"		Create a Collage Quiz	
* Tape 5 teachers/friends	/5	* 12 x 18 in.	/5
* Written instructions for participants	/5	* 15 target vocabulary words	/5
* 2 actions per teacher/friend	/5	* 15 illustrations in color	/5
* Narration with descriptive sentences	/5	* Neatly written or typed	/5
* Play video for class	/5	* Answer key on reverse	/5
Total points	/25	**Total points**	/25

Write a Story		Write a Diary or Journal Entry	
* 2-3 paragraphs	/5	* Daily entries in target language	/5
* Min. 10 target words	/5	* Use journal/diary format	/5
* Must have a theme/plot	/5	* Date and day of week for every entry	/5
* Neatly written or typed	/5	* Min. 2 sentences per day	/5
* Correct spelling and grammar	/5	* Neatly written or typed	/5
Total points	/25	**Total points**	/25

Show your project choices to your teacher by: _____

All of your projects are due on: _____

Differentiated Instruction for World Languages   ©2013 Hubbert and Nieminen

Technology

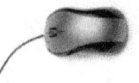

Choose two projects to complete.

Send an E-mail

Send an e-mail to your teacher. Ask what are his/her favorite electronic items, movies, books, and hobbies.

Survey and Graph

Survey classmates using the target language about the technology items they own. Create an Excel spreadsheet with a graph.

Write Instructions for Internet Map Programs

Write simple instructions on how to use Google Maps or MapQuest using target language.

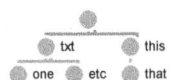

Research Growth of Technology

Research growth of technology in the target country. Write an informational article or create a poster. May be computer generated.

Create a 3-D Museum Exhibit

Create an exhibit of early to modern communication devices in the target country.

Create a Facebook Page

Create a Facebook page for inventor(s) from the target country who have made contributions to technological advances.

Create a Cartoon

Create an original cartoon about technology or an electronic item of your choosing. Choose still-life or animation.

Create a "Post-It" note Flipbook

Create a "Post-It" note flipbook about target country technology using electronics vocabulary.

Your Choice!

Technology Assessment Rubric

Send an E-mail	
* Subject line: Your name and class	____/5
* Ask 4 questions in target language	____/5
* Must be complete sentences	____/5
* Pick one and ask why it is teacher's favorite	____/5
* Last reply includes thank you	____/5
Total points	____/25

Survey and Graph	
* Survey 7-10 classmates	____/5
* Excel in proper format	____/5
* Graph created from the Excel	____/5
* Use color in graph	____/5
* Share with the class	____/5
Total points	____/25

Write Instructions for Internet Map Programs	
* Min. 5 steps/instructions	____/5
* Number each step	____/5
* In target language	____/5
* Computer generated with graphics	____/5
* Submit electronically to teacher	____/5
Total points	____/25

Research Growth of Technology	
* Include 3-5 methods of technology	____/5
* Min. 5 visuals/graphics	____/5
* Computer generated	____/5
* Appropriate title	____/5
* Author name immediately after title	____/5
Total points	____/25

Create a 3-D Museum Exhibit	
* Must be 3-D	____/5
* Min. ten 3-D objects	____/5
* Each item labeled	____/5
* Labels must be in target language	____/5
* Present to class	____/5
Total points	____/25

Create a Facebook Page	
* Use Facebook template	____/5
* Photo/illustration of inventor	____/5
* Photo/illustration of invention	____/5
* Brief description of invention	____/5
* Bio of inventor	____/5
Total points	____/25

Create a Cartoon	
* 6-8 frames and 8.5 x 11 in. drawn, min. 15 seconds animated	____/5
* Must be in color	____/5
* All dialogue/words in target language	____/5
* Each frame must include words	____/5
* Title and author in first frame	____/5
Total points	____/25

Create a "Post-It" note Flipbook	
* Min. 25 post-it notes	____/5
* Min. 5 vocabulary terms	____/5
* Illustrations on every page	____/5
* Understandable theme	____/5
* Front cover with title and name	____/5
Total points	____/25

_____!	
	____/5
	____/5
	____/5
	____/5
	____/5
Total points	____/25

Show your project choices to your teacher by:

All of your projects are due on:

Differentiated Instruction for World Languages ©2013 Hubbert and Nieminen

Unit 5: Score with Grammar

- Teacher Tips for Pages 72 to 79 71
- Nouns 72
- Adjectives 74
- Pronouns: Formal and Informal 76
- Verbs 78
- Teacher Tips for Pages 81 to 84 80
- Exclamations, Questions, and Declarative Sentences 81
- Likes and Dislikes 83

Teacher Tips for Pages 72 to 79

Standards

Nouns

1.3	1.3	1.3
1.3	3.1/Tech	1.3
1.3	1.3	1.3
1.3	1.3	

Adjectives

1.3	1.3/Art	1.3
1.1	1.2	1.3
4.1	1.3	

Pronouns: formal and informal

1.3	1.3	1.3
1.3	3.1/ELA	1.3
1.3	1.3	3.1/ELA
3.1/Music	1.3	3.2

Verbs

1.3	1.3	1.3
1.3	3.1/Art	3.1/Tech
3.1/Art	1.3	1.3
1.3	3.1/Drama	1.3

- ❖ **Preview Material**
    - ○ For videotaped or recorded products, it is always wise to preview the video or recording prior to class presentation
- ❖ **Nouns**
    - ○ For those students who choose "Be the Teacher," ensure that they are aware of time limits (that you set) as well as having all materials ready to be copied at least one day prior to the presentation.
- ❖ **Adjectives**
    - ○ Ideas for "Your Choice": Create a song about all the colors of the rainbow. Write a poem using at least 15 adjectives on a subject of your choice.
- ❖ **Pronouns**
    - ○ Review the elements of a well-developed paragraph prior to assigning projects.
- ❖ **Verbs**
    - ○ See reference pages for *More Verb Activities* on page 114.

Easy Grading for *Score 100* menu:
This menu requires students selecting one or more projects which add up to *Score 100*. To keep the assessment simple, the rubrics use the same point value (25) as the others. To calculate the final grade for each student, determine the percentage of points earned.
EXAMPLE 1: Student A has chosen the 20, 30, and 50 *Score 100*-projects from the menu. Student A has received 60 out of 75 on the assessment rubric. To determine overall percentage, divide 60 by 75. The student has earned an 80% for a grade.
EXAMPLE 2: Student B has chosen the 20 and 80 *Score 100*-projects and has received a total of 45 out of 50 on the assessment rubric. Divide 45 by 50; student has earned a 90% for a grade.

Nouns

Score 100 ~ Gain yards with Football
1. Select any combination of yards to total 100.
2. Mark your choices and show your teacher by: _____.
3. All projects are due by: _____.

20 Yard Run

Create a Brochure
- Create a brochure about nouns. Include 10 nouns and the rules of definite articles. Use target language vocabulary.

Create a Store Sales Flyer
- Create a store sales flyer using target vocabulary with a minimum of 10 items.

Construct a Mobile
- Construct a mobile using target vocabulary and illustrations with 10-20 nouns.

Design a Collage
- Design a collage of noun vocabulary. Include answer key on reverse side of collage.

30 Yard Field Goal

Produce a Videotaped Commercial
- Produce a videotaped commercial using noun vocabulary.

Create a Bingo Game
- Create a bingo game with target vocabulary. Include minimum of 40 vocabulary words.

Make Themed Flashcards
- Make 2 sets of themed flashcards.

50 Yard "Hail Mary"

Design a Crossword Puzzle and a Word Search
- Design a crossword puzzle and a word search for your classmates to solve using target vocabulary. May be computer generated.

Create a Class Activity/Game
- Create a Class Activity/Game to memorize noun vocabulary.

Design a Bulletin Board Display
- Design and craft a bulletin board display titled "All about Nouns." Include pictures, labels, and descriptive sentences, etc.

100 Yard Touchdown

Be the Teacher
- Teach nouns to the class; include worksheet, visuals, homework assignment, and class activity.

Nouns Assessment Rubric

Create a Brochure		Create a Store Sales Flyer		Construct a Mobile	
* 8.5 x 11 in., folded	___/5	* Min. 8.5 x 11 in.	___/5	* 10-20 nouns	___/5
* 10 nouns with correct definite article	___/5	* Min. 10 items	___/5	* Correctly spelled labels	___/5
* Must have pictures and written information	___/5	* Sale and original price included	___/5	* 2-3 hanging levels	___/5
* Name on the back	___/5	* Illustrate each item in color	___/5	* Illustrations in color	___/5
* Neatly written and drawn or computer generated	___/5	* Neatly written or computer generated	___/5	* Must be balanced	___/5
Total points	___/25	**Total points**	___/25	**Total Points**	___/25

Design a Collage		Produce a Videotaped Commercial		Create a Bingo Game	
* 12 x 18 in.	___/5	* Min. 1 minute long	___/5	* Set of 40 vocabulary cards, words neatly written	___/5
* Correctly labeled in target language	___/5	* Min. 10 items	___/5	* Make 5 bingo cards using template	___/5
* Appropriate title for collage	___/5	* Min. 1 visual aid per item	___/5	* Illustrations in color for each square	___/5
* Select 20 themed nouns (e.g. clothing, food, school)	___/5	* Store name with slogan included	___/5	* Adequate volume when leading game	___/5
* Answer key with student name on the back	___/5	* Clear pronunciation required	___/5	* Lead the game	___/5
Total points	___/25	**Total points**	___/25	**Total Points**	___/25

Make Themed Flashcards		Design Puzzles		Create a Class Activity	
* 3 x 5 in. index cards	___/5	* 20 different nouns for each puzzle	___/5	* Entire class must be able to participate	___/5
* 2 sets, min. 20 nouns each set	___/5	* Create appropriate clues for each puzzle	___/5	* Simple rules with answer key	___/5
* Illustrations in color	___/5	* Include puzzles and answer key	___/5	* Approved by teacher prior to play	___/5
* Label on reverse side of illustration	___/5	* Classmates must be able to solve puzzles	___/5	* Provide all required objects for play	___/5
* Container or carrying bag for cards	___/5	* Turn in solved and corrected puzzles	___/5	* Lead the game	___/5
Total points	___/25	**Total points**	___/25	**Total points**	___/25

Design a Bulletin Board		Be the Teacher	
* Min. 15 vocabulary words	___/5	* List of 20 nouns	___/5
* Must be in target language	___/5	* Worksheet in creative format	___/5
* Colored illustrations with labels	___/5	* Fun and appropriate class activity	___/5
* Descriptive sentence for each noun	___/5	* Relevant homework assignment	___/5
* Neat and creative	___/5	* Visuals in color	___/5
Total points	___/25	**Total points**	___/25

Adjectives

Choose two projects to complete.

Find Adjectives

Find an adjective for each letter or character of the alphabet in the target language.

Draw Adjectives

Draw at least 10 adjectives and write a descriptive phrase for each.

Design an Award

Design an award for your best friend. Describe the award in detail with at least 10 adjectives using the target language.

Describe a Character

Describe a character from a book you are reading. Share your character description with the class.

Find New Adjectives

Use the dictionary to find 10 new adjectives and use them in sentences.

Create a Children's Book

Write and illustrate a children's book of adjectives and/or colors.

Complete a Venn Diagram

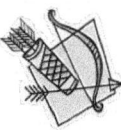

Compare two items or people, e.g. cats/dogs, you/your brother, two friends, etc. Use the target language.

Describe a Teacher or a Friend

Describe your favorite teacher or best friend. Use complete sentences in the target language.

Your Choice!

Adjectives Assessment Rubric

Find Adjectives		Draw Adjectives		Design an Award	
* 8.5 x 11 in.	___/5	* 8.5 x 11 in.	___/5	* Drawn or 3-D	___/5
* Illustrate a min. of 10 adjectives	___/5	* Use target language	___/5	* 8.5 x 11 in. drawing, min. 10 in. tall for 3-D	___/5
* List in alphabetical order	___/5	* Correct grammar	___/5	* Description of award with min. 10 adjectives	___/5
* Neatly written or computer generated	___/5	* Use correct form of adjective in the phrase	___/5	* Correct use of adjectives	___/5
* Correct spelling	___/5	* Must be in color	___/5	* Read description aloud to class	___/5
Total points	___/25	**Total points**	___/25	**Total Points**	___/25

Describe a Character		Find New Adjectives		Create a Children's Book	
* Neatly written or typed in the target language	___/5	* Min. 8.5 x 11 in.	___/5	* Min. 5 x 7 in., bound	___/5
* Photo or illustration of character	___/5	* 10 new adjectives	___/5	* 10 illustrated pages in color	___/5
* Include title of book and author in description	___/5	* Illustrate 5 in color	___/5	* Use min. 10 adjectives/ colors	___/5
* Include min. 10 adjectives in description	___/5	* Neatly written or computer generated in the target language	___/5	* Neatly written or computer generated in the target language	___/5
* Name of character as title	___/5	* Correct sentence structure	___/5	* Title page with author name	___/5
Total points	___/25	**Total points**	___/25	**Total points**	___/25

Complete a Venn Diagram		Describe a Teacher or a Friend		_____!	
* 8.5 x 11 in.	___/5	* Min. 1 minute long	___/5		___/5
* Two comparisons	___/5	* Script for teacher review prior to speech	___/5		___/5
* Min. 15 adjectives	___/5	* Create the award/trophy in 3-D	___/5		___/5
* Use color and designs to enhance diagram	___/5	* Delivered with appropriate volume and excitement	___/5		___/5
* Title Venn and label sections	___/5	* Quality of presentation (practice is evident)	___/5		___/5
Total points	___/25	**Total points**	___/25	**Total points**	___/25

Show your project choices to your teacher by: _____

All of your projects are due on: _____

Pronouns: Formal and Informal

Score 100 ~ Qualify for Pole Position
1. Select any combination of laps to total 100.
2. Mark your choices and show your teacher by: _____.
3. All projects are due by: _____.

20 Laps

- **Make Flashcards** in the 1st, 2nd, and 3rd person singular and plural pronouns.
- **Make a Poster** containing pronouns in English and the target language.
- **Design Greeting Cards:** one formal, one informal in the target language. Use a minimum of three different verbs.
- **Write 10 Sentences** using pronouns in the target language.

50 Laps

- **Write a Well-Developed Paragraph in English** explaining the informal and formal expressions in the target country.
- **Create a Magazine Cover** with photos; use informal and formal pronouns in the target language.
- **Create a PowerPoint Game** using pronouns in the target language.

80 Laps

- **Create Three Dialogues** using informal and formal expressions to introduce friends and business colleagues.
- **Write a Well-Developed Paragraph in the Target Language** explaining informal and formal expressions in the target country.
- **Create a Song/ Rap** using all the pronouns of the target language.

100 Laps

- **Write a Skit about Pronouns** Include appropriate verb forms.
- **Conduct Two Interviews:** one formal and one informal. "Interview" the president/leader and a citizen of the target country. Use target language.

Pronouns: Formal and Informal Assessment Rubric

Make Flashcards		Make a Poster		Design Greeting Cards	
* 3 x 5 in. index cards	__/5	* Standard poster size	__/5	* 5 x 7 in. each card	__/5
* All required elements included	__/5	* Neat and creative, legible	__/5	* Correct use of pronouns and verbs	__/5
* English on one side, target language on the other	__/5	* All pronouns included	__/5	* Neatly written and drawn or computer generated	__/5
* Include container or carrying bag for cards	__/5	* Appropriate title	__/5	* Trademark and student name on the back	__/5
* Play game with partner	__/5	* Use color	__/5	* Illustrations in color	__/5
Total points	__/25	**Total points**	__/25	**Total Points**	__/25
Write 10 Sentences		**Write a Paragraph in English**		**Create a Magazine Cover**	
* Numbered sentences	__/5	* Min. 7-10 sentences	__/5	* 8.5 x 11 in.	__/5
* Use different pronouns and verbs	__/5	* Title with author name immediately following	__/5	* Use informal and formal pronouns	__/5
* Neatly written or typed	__/5	* Typed, double-spaced, max. size 14 font	__/5	* 5 photos or illustrations	__/5
* Correct spelling and structure	__/5	* Sufficient supporting details	__/5	* Magazine must have title	__/5
* Read to class	__/5	* Topic sentence	__/5	* Layout enhances topics	__/5
Total points	__/25	**Total points**	__/25	**Total Points**	__/25
Create a PowerPoint Game		**Create Three Dialogues**		**Write a Paragraph in Target Language**	
* Min. 10 numbered slides	__/5	* Min. 3-4 lines per dialogue	__/5	* Min. 7-10 sentences	__/5
* Include all subject pronouns	__/5	* Pronouns used in each dialogue	__/5	* Title with author name immediately following	__/5
* Simple rules on separate slide	__/5	* Copy to teacher for review prior to performance	__/5	* Sufficient supporting details	__/5
* Separate title slide	__/5	* Neatly written or typed	__/5	* Topic sentence	__/5
* Lead the game	__/5	* Perform with a classmate	__/5	* Typed, double-spaced, max. size 14 font	__/5
Total points	__/25	**Total points**	__/25	**Total points**	__/25
Create a Song or a Rap		**Write a Skit about Pronouns**		**Conduct Two Interviews**	
* 1-2 minutes long	__/5	* 3-5 minutes long in the target language	__/5	* "Interview" the president or leader of the target country	__/5
* Written words for teacher review prior to performance	__/5	* Use all subject pronouns with correct verb forms	__/5	* "Interview" a citizen of the target country	__/5
* Must have melody	__/5	* Copy of written script to teacher prior to performance	__/5	* Neatly written or typed	__/5
* All pronouns included	__/5	* Correct and clear pronunciation during skit	__/5	* 10 questions per each interviewee w/ answers	__/5
* Perform live or play recording	__/5	* Perform for class	__/5	* Perform interviews for class with a classmate	__/5
Total points	__/25	**Total points**	__/25	**Total points**	__/25

Verbs

Score 100 ~ Run, Jump or Throw for a Gold Medal
1. Select any combination of events to score 100.
2. Mark your choices and show your teacher by: _____.
3. All projects are due by: _____.

Discus 20

- **Make a Poster** of verbs by drawing or using magazine pictures.
- **Conduct a Magazine Verb Search** Find an article about the target country and translate verbs to target language.
- **Sequence Events** using verbs in preparation for your gold medal party.

High Jump 30

- **Write Sentences** comparing what you do and what your teacher does during a day. Use target language.
- **Photograph Several People** *doing something*, and then label each photo with the appropriate verb in the target language.

Javelin 50

- **Videotape and Narrate** friends and family doing different things. Film as many natural occurrences as possible. Two activities per person. Use target vocabulary. Editing is a must.
- **Sculpt People or Animals** using clay or wire; demonstrate 10 verbs in your choice of medium. Write a sentence for each in the target language using "place cards."

Relay 80

- **Write a Commercial** to sell a product. E.g. exercise equipment, car, motorcycle, etc. Use target language.
- **Write a Journal Entry** Five entries for each: yesterday, today, tomorrow. Use correct verb tenses.
- **Write a "How To" Card** Try to use as many verbs as possible. The card can be for a fake item, but the item should be usable; e.g. "Alien catcher."

Marathon 100

- **Write and Act Out a Play** about verbs in the target language.
- **Be the Teacher** Teach verbs to the class; include visuals, a verb vocabulary list, a homework assignment, and a class activity.

Verbs Assessment Rubric

Make a Poster		Conduct a Magazine Verb Search		Sequence Events	
* Standard poster size	/5	* Find min. 20 verbs	/5	* Min. 10 events	/5
* Min. 20 labeled verbs	/5	* Underline all verbs	/5	* Numbered events	/5
* Color illustrations	/5	* List in alphabetical order	/5	* Neatly written or typed in the target language	/5
* Use the target language	/5	* Translate verbs from English to target language	/5	* Correct verb conjugation	/5
* Include an appropriate title	/5	* Neatly written or typed	/5	* Make invitation to party	/5
Total points	/25	**Total points**	/25	**Total Points**	/25
Write Sentences		**Photograph Several People**		**Videotape and Narrate**	
* 10 action verbs	/5	* 10 photos	/5	* Min. 10 verbs	/5
* Numbered sentences	/5	* Photos must be printed	/5	* Min. 2 minutes long	/5
* Correct verb conjugation	/5	* Label each photo with appropriate verb	/5	* Correct pronunciation	/5
* Neatly written or typed	/5	* Correct spelling	/5	* Use complete sentences	/5
* Read sentences to class	/5	* Display in a format of your choice	/5	* Taping is of good quality	/5
Total points	/25	**Total points**	/25	**Total Points**	/25
Sculpt People or Animals		**Write a Commercial**		**Write a Journal Entry**	
* 10 verbs	/5	* 30-60 seconds long	/5	* Min. 15 entries in the target language	/5
* Min. 4 in. height	/5	* Must have the product	/5	* Neatly written or typed	/5
* Clay or wire in 3-D	/5	* Written dialogue to teacher prior to performance	/5	* Include day and date	/5
* Correct verb structure	/5	* Adequate volume and correct pronunciation	/5	* Complete sentences in 1st person	/5
* Sentence on "place cards"	/5	* Perform live or play video	/5	* Correct verb tenses	/5
Total points	/25	**Total points**	/25	**Total Points**	/25
Write a "How-To" Card		**Write and Act Out a Play**		**Be the Teacher**	
* Min. 5 x 7 in. card	/5	* 1-2 minutes long	/5	* Verbs vocabulary list with 15 verbs	/5
* Min. 10 verbs	/5	* Min. 15 verbs	/5	* Supporting visuals must be used	/5
* Illustrations support instructions	/5	* Script turned in to teacher prior to performance	/5	* Relevant homework assignment	/5
* Provides clear instructions in target language	/5	* Props and costumes	/5	* Fun class activity	/5
* Numbered steps	/5	* Live performance	/5	* Well-prepared and creative	/5
Total points	/25	**Total points**	/25	**Total Points**	/25

Differentiated Instruction for World Languages ©2013 Hubbert and Nieminen

Teacher Tips for Pages 81 to 84

Standards

Exclamations, Questions, and Declarative Sentences

1.3	1.3
3.1/Art	1.2
3.1/Tech	1.3
1.3	1.3
5.1	1.3

Likes and Dislikes Page 1

1.1	1.3	1.1
1.3/Tech	1.1	1.3
1.1	1.3	

Likes and Dislikes Page 2

1.1/ELA	1.1	1.1
1.3	1.3	3.1/Music

- ❖ **Preview Material**
  - o For videotaped or recorded products, it is always wise to preview the video or recording prior to class presentation.
- ❖ **Exclamations, Questions, and Declarative Sentences**
  - o The *Ice-skating* column is lower level than the *Hockey* column.
  - o In the assessment rubric, the assessment with *both* the ice-skate and hockey-skate apply to *Write True and False Sentences*.
  - o Options for extra projects:

  - Using a "facial expressions chart," Write Descriptive Remarks using correct exclamatory sentences.

  - Compile a Collage of question words.

  - You Be the Teacher; teach correct structure for simple declarative sentences.

  - Create a Chart illustrating affirmative and negative sentences using appropriate sentence format.

  - Create a Quiz about question words for your classmates to solve. Include an answer key.

  - Write 10 Statements about a subject of your choice. E.g. family, friends, school, etc.

- ❖ **Likes and dislikes**
  - o Due to the written and computer-generated content requirements, additional computer time may be necessary.
  - o See page 71 for easy grading for *Score 100*-menu.

Exclamations, Questions, and Declarative Sentences

Skate around the Rink
1. Choose a total of three projects to complete from the *Ice Skating* and/or the *Hockey* columns.
2. One project needs to be chosen from each category in either column: Exclamations, questions, and declarative sentences.
3. Mark your choices and show your teacher by: _____.
4. All projects are due by: _____.

 Ice Skating

Exclamations

- Make Flashcards illustrating the target command vocabulary.
- Create a Children's Book using affirmative and negative sentences.

Questions

- Create a Poster of all the question words in the target language.
- Write Questions and Answers using all of the question words.

Declarative Sentences

- Create a PowerPoint describing your favorite places using pictures and statements.
- Write True and False Sentences about the target country culture for a quiz.

 **Hockey**

Exclamations

- Find 15 pictures in magazines and Write Descriptive Exclamations using complete sentences.
- Create 10 New Commands and instruct your classmates to do the commands.

Questions

- Create a Questionnaire and Interview a classmate or a target language speaker.
- Draw a Cartoon/Comic with a storyline using question words.

Declarative Sentences

- Write 10 Declarative Sentences using your current vocabulary list.
- Write True and False Sentences on a subject of your choice using the target language.

Exclamations, Questions, and Declarative Sentences Assessment Rubric

Make Flashcards		Create a Children's Book	
3 x 5 in. index cards	___/5	5 x 7 in., bound	___/5
20 commands	___/5	10 pages with 1 sentence on each page	___/5
Illustration on one side, target language command on the other	___/5	Neatly drawn, written in the target language	___/5
Container or carrying bag	___/5	Illustrations in color	___/5
Play with a partner	___/5	Title page with author name	___/5
Total points	___/25	**Total points**	___/25

Create a Poster		Write Questions and Answers	
Standard poster size	___/5	Number each question and answer	___/5
Illustrations with sample questions	___/5	Q & A must make sense	___/5
Neatly written and drawn	___/5	Neatly written or typed in the target language	___/5
Title and correct spelling	___/5	Correct spelling and structure	___/5
Must be in color	___/5	Present to class	___/5
Total points	___/25	**Total points**	___/25

Create a PowerPoint		Write True and False Sentences	
10 content slides	___/5	10-15 T/F statements	___/5
Color graphic(s) and words on each slide	___/5	Target country or subject of choice	___/5
Use target language	___/5	Title your quiz or statements	___/5
Title slide with student name	___/5	Typed and numbered statements	___/5
Imaginative descriptions	___/5	Answer key included	___/5
Total points	___/25	**Total points**	___/25

Write Descriptive or Declarative Sentences		Create 10 New Commands	
15 sentences	___/5	10 commands in the target language	___/5
Correct spelling and structure	___/5	Ability to execute command	___/5
Include picture next to each sentence	___/5	Neatly written or typed	___/5
Neatly written or typed in target language	___/5	Copy to teacher prior to instruction	___/5
Read to class	___/5	Present to class	___/5
Total points	___/25	**Total points**	___/25

Create Questionnaire and Interview		Draw a Cartoon/Comic	
10 questions	___/5	8.5 x 11 in.	___/5
Questionnaire for teacher review	___/5	6 frames	___/5
Neatly written or typed	___/5	Each frame with dialogue and/or text	___/5
Q & A written out in the target language	___/5	In target language	___/5
Read to class	___/5	Must be in color	___/5
Total points	___/25	**Total points**	___/25

Likes and Dislikes

Score 100 ~ Win Match Point with Volleyball
1. Select any combination of hits or passes to total 100.
2. Mark your choices and show your teacher by: _____.
3. All projects are due by: _____.

Serve for 20

- **List Five** of your likes and five of your dislikes. Use complete sentences.
- **Chart 10 Things** you like/do not like to do.
- **Create a Brochure** of your favorite/least favorite foods using target vocabulary.

Volley for 30

- **Videotape and Narrate** 10 things you like/do not like to do.
- **Write to Express (A)** what your classmates like/dislike in the 3rd person singular using target vocabulary.
- **Write to Express (B)** what your classmates like to do/don't like to do in the 3rd person plural using target vocabulary.

Dig for 50

- **Survey Likes and Dislikes** of at least 10 classmates. Tally on a poster.
- **Make a Wish Chart** using the phrase "I would like to..." in the target language.
- **Create a Scrapbook** of likes and dislikes using target vocabulary.

Spike for 80

- **Recommend a Book** or a movie to a friend using the likes/dislikes vocabulary.
- **Present Your Point of View** using target vocabulary.
- **You Are the Judge** of a fashion show or food fair. Tell us your likes/dislikes.

Ace for 100

- **Invent a New Ice Cream Flavor** Tell everyone why your new flavor is the best.
- **Design a Magazine Cover** and create a full page ad in the back cover using likes/dislikes vocabulary.
- **Write a Song** in the target language about likes and dislikes.

Likes and Dislikes Assessment Rubric

List Five		Chart 10 Things		Create a Brochure	
* Five likes	/5	* 10 likes/dislikes	/5	* 8.5 x 11 in., folded	/5
* Five dislikes	/5	* Chart format	/5	* Front cover with title	/5
* Complete sentences in the target language	/5	* Complete sentences in the target language	/5	* Illustrations in color	/5
* Neatly written or typed	/5	* Neatly written or computer generated	/5	* Neatly written and drawn or computer generated	/5
* Illustrate each like and dislike	/5	* Share with class	/5	* Creativity counts	/5
Total points	/25	**Total points**	/25	**Total Points**	/25
Videotape and Narrate		**Write to Express, (A) and (B)**		**Survey Likes and Dislikes**	
* Include both likes and dislikes	/5	* 10 typed sentences	/5	* Standard poster size	/5
* Narrate video in target language	/5	* Correct grammar and spelling	/5	* Survey 10 classmates in the target language	/5
* Use complete sentences	/5	* Complete sentences	/5	* Both likes and dislikes included	/5
* Clear volume and pronunciation	/5	* Use 3rd person singular for (A), 3rd person plural for (B)	/5	* Title your work	/5
* Share video with class	/5	* Read to class	/5	* Use color to enhance results	/5
Total points	/25	**Total points**	/25	**Total points**	/25
Make a Wish Chart		**Create a Scrapbook**			
* 10 wishes with title	/5	* Min. 5 x 7 in., bound	/5		
* Copy of written phrases to teacher	/5	* Min. 10 pages	/5		
* Use color in chart	/5	* Both likes/dislikes included	/5		
* Min. 1 illustration	/5	* Illustrations in color (drawings, magazine or internet pictures)	/5		
* Creative presentation method	/5	* Title cover with student name	/5		
Total points	/25	**Total points**	/25		

Assessments continue on the next page

Differentiated Instruction for World Languages ©2013 Hubbert and Nieminen

Likes and Dislikes Assessment Rubric

Recommend a Book		Present Your Point of View		You are the Judge	
* 1-3 paragraphs, typed	____/5	* 1-3 paragraphs	____/5	* 10 likes/dislikes	____/5
* Title includes name of book & author or movie & director	____/5	* Use one topic only	____/5	* Chart format	____/5
* Correct spelling and grammar	____/5	* Title with student name immediately following	____/5	* Complete sentences in the target language	____/5
* Min. 1 graphic referring to book or movie	____/5	* Typed, double-spaced, max. size 14 font	____/5	* Neatly written or computer generated	____/5
* Present to class	____/5	* Read to class	____/5	* Share with class	____/5
Total points	____/25	**Total points**	____/25	**Total Points**	____/25

Invent a New Ice-Cream Flavor		Design a Magazine Cover		Write a Song	
* Name the flavor	____/5	* Appropriate title	____/5	* 1-2 minutes long	____/5
* 1-3 paragraphs	____/5	* Likes and dislikes used in layout	____/5	* Must have melody	____/5
* Well-developed paragraphs in target language	____/5	* Graphics/illustrations in color	____/5	* Min. 15 vocabulary words	____/5
* Include location (where people can buy it) and price	____/5	* Neatly written and drawn or computer generated	____/5	* Written words for teacher review prior to performance	____/5
* Colored illustration(s)	____/5	* Back cover ad must fill entire page	____/5	* Perform live or play recording	____/5
Total points	____/25	**Total points**	____/25	**Total points**	____/25

Unit 6: Going Places

- ❖ Teacher Tips for Pages 88 to 95 87
- ❖ Going to the Market 88
- ❖ Choose Your Ticket: Sporting Events, Concerts, Bus and Train Rides 90
- ❖ Vacation and Travel 92
- ❖ Visiting or Obtaining Services from Community Service Programs 94
- ❖ Teacher Tips for Pages 97 to 103 96
- ❖ Shopping Experience 97
- ❖ Eating Out 99
- ❖ Public and Private Schools 102

Teacher Tips for Pages 88 - 95

Standards

Going to the Market

4.1	2.2	1.3
1.3		2.1
1.3	1.3	3.1/Math

› **Challenge 1:** 1.3
› **Challenge 2:** 2.2

Choose Your Ticket:
Sporting events, Concerts, Bus and Train rides

All Projects
4.2/Art/ELA

Vacation and Travel

2.1	2.1	1.3
1.3	1.3	3.1/ELA
4.2	4.2	3.1/ELA

› **Challenge 1:** 3.2
› **Challenge 2:** 5.1

Community Services Programs

3.1/S.S.	1.1
4.2	4.2
3.2	1.3

❖ **Preview Material**
  o For videotaped or recorded products, it is always wise to preview the video or recording prior to class presentation.
❖ **Going to the Market**
  o If possible, purchase authentic food items from your local ethnic grocery store or online. Downloading photos and laminating the printed material would also be beneficial for student involvement.
❖ **Choose Your Ticket** is a Teacher's Choice. See page 34 for Teacher's Choice explanation.
❖ **Vacation and Travel**
  o Order travel brochures online or visit a travel agency and raid its selection.
  o Another version of "Choose Your Ticket": Set up a travel agency in your classroom. Students create dialogues to ask about travel destinations, purchase tickets, etc.
❖ **Community Service Programs** is a Teacher's Choice. See page 34 for Teacher's Choice explanation.
  o If possible, have copies of maps available for student use, especially city and state/province maps of the target country.

Going to the Market

Select "Three-in-a-Row" to complete the tic-tac-toe.

Describe Five Fruits and Five Vegetables Describe five fruits and five vegetables using target vocabulary and at least one adjective for each product.	Illustrate a Cereal Box Illustrate a cereal box from the target country. Write a 2-3 sentence description.	Draw a Map Draw a map of the grocery store/market place. Include aisle and product descriptions in the target language. 
Write a Grocery List Write a grocery list using target vocabulary.	Your Choice! 	Create a Menu Create a menu list of target country menu items for breakfast, lunch, and dinner. Use target language.
Construct a Mobile Construct a mobile of 10 food items with labels. 	Write a Dialogue Write a dialogue for the market place; ask the clerk questions and include your answers. Use target vocabulary.	Survey with a Graph Survey your classmates about their favorite foods. Give them a minimum of five to choose from and then graph the results.

➢ **Challenge 1:** Write Out a Menu in the target language for a birthday party using products found at the market.

➢ **Challenge 2:** Create a 30-second Commercial about a product you would find at the market. Use target language.

Write Out a Menu		Create a 30-second Commercial	
* Shopping list of 20 products	___ / 5	* 30 seconds min.	___ / 5
* 5 menu items	___ / 5	* Include slogan	___ / 5
* Illustrations in color	___ / 5	* Script for teacher review prior to performance	___ / 5
* Name of party, date and time, etc.	___ / 5	* Product, prop(s), costume(s)	___ / 5
* Creative presentation format (e.g. poster)	___ / 5	* Perform live or play video	___ / 5
Total points	___ / 25	**Total points**	___ / 25

Going to the Market Assessment Rubric

Describe Five Fruits and Five Vegetables		Illustrate a Cereal Box		Draw a Map	
* 5 fruits	/5	* Approx. 9 x 11 x 2 in.	/5	* 8.5 x 11 in.	/5
* 5 vegetables	/5	* Must use target language	/5	* Name the store	/5
* Use complete sentences	/5	* Must be in color	/5	* Include aisle descriptions	/5
* Min. 1 adjective per product	/5	* Must have both words and illustrations	/5	* Label 10 product locations	/5
* Neatly written or typed	/5	* Description of product on front cover	/5	* Use color	/5
Total points	/25	**Total points**	/25	**Total Points**	/25

Write a Grocery List		_____!		Create a Menu	
* 8.5 x 11 in.	/5		/5	* 5 breakfast items	/5
* 20 items min.	/5		/5	* 5 lunch items	/5
* Buy for a special occasion	/5		/5	* 5 dinner items	/5
* Create an illustrated border	/5		/5	* 1 Illustration per meal	/5
* Neatly written or computer generated	/5		/5	* Neatly written and drawn or computer generated	/5
Total points	/25	**Total points**	/25	**Total points**	/25

Construct a Mobile		Write a Dialogue		Survey with a Graph	
* 10 food items	/5	* Min. 10 vocabulary words	/5	* Min. 5 choices	/5
* Correctly labeled in the target language	/5	* Min. 5 questions	/5	* Survey in target language	/5
* Illustrations in color (drawings, magazine or internet pictures)	/5	* Min. 5 responses	/5	* Title and correct graph format	/5
* Must be balanced	/5	* Neatly written or typed	/5	* Use color in the graph	/5
* Display in classroom	/5	* Perform for class	/5	* Turn in original tally sheet to teacher with project	/5
Total points	/25	**Total points**	/25	**Total points**	/25

Show your project choices to your teacher by: _____

All of your projects are due on: _____

Differentiated Instruction for World Languages ©2013 Hubbert and Nieminen

Choose Your Ticket!
Sporting Events, Concerts, Bus and Train Rides
~ Teacher's Choice

Instructions:
1. Students are divided into 4 equal groups.
2. Groups: train, bus, concert, sports event.
3. Each student in a group will choose an activity to complete.
4. Paper money and coins will be made by each group.

How to play:
1. Choose venue and create stations
2. One person at ticket counter with tickets and money
3. 2-3 customers with money
4. Students use appropriate dialogue to buy/sell tickets.

Make Tickets for Sporting Events
Create tickets for a sporting event. Prices need to be in target country currency. Use a variety of prices. Name the sporting events and include dates, and times.

Create a Program for a Sporting Event
1. 8.5 x 11 in., folded
2. Illustrated front cover in color with title of event, date, and time
3. Neatly written and drawn or computer generated
4. List of events
5. Use target country sporting events

Make Tickets for Concerts
Create tickets for concerts. Prices need to be in target country currency. Use a variety of prices. Name the concerts and include dates, and times.

Create a Program for a Concert
1. 8.5 x 11 in., folded
2. Illustrated front cover in color with title of event, date, and time
3. Neatly written and drawn or computer generated
4. List of target country performers
5. Use target language

Make Paper Money in the target country currency
1. Min. 5 x maximum amount of ticket price
2. Large variety of denominations
3. Min. 50 bills in color
4. Target country currency
5. Cut out individually

Make Coins in the target country currency
1. Min. 75 coins
2. Large variety of coins
3. Cardboard or heavy paper
4. Target country currency
5. Cut out individually

Make Train or Bus Tickets
Create tickets for the train or the bus. Prices need to be in target country currency. Use a variety of prices. Include the train and bus names, dates and times.

Create a Train or Bus Schedule
1. Each schedule: 8.5 x 11 in., folded
2. Include departures and destinations
3. Min. 1 graphic/illustration
4. Include times and days
5. Neatly written or computer generated

Choose Your Ticket Assessment Rubric
Sporting Events, Concerts, Bus and Train Rides

Make Tickets for Sporting Events		Make Paper Money in the target country currency		Create a Program for a Sporting Event	
* Prices in target country currency	/5	* Correct ticket prices	/5	* 8.5 x 11 in., folded	/5
* Min. 15 tickets	/5	* Min. 50 bills in color	/5	* Illustrated front cover with title of event, date, and time	/5
* Use a variety of prices	/5	* Target country currency	/5	* List of events	/5
* Name of sporting events	/5	* Large variety of denominations	/5	* Use target country sporting events	/5
* Dates and times in target language	/5	* Bills cut out individually	/5	* Neatly written or computer generated	/5
Total points	/25	**Total points**	/25	**Total Points**	/25

Make Coins in the target country currency		Make Tickets for Concerts		Make Train or Bus Tickets	
* Min. 75 coins	/5	* Min. 15 tickets	/5	* Min. 15 tickets each	/5
* Target country currency	/5	* Prices in target country currency	/5	* Prices in target country currency	/5
* Large variety of coins	/5	* Use a variety of prices	/5	* Use a variety of prices	/5
* Use cardboard or heavy paper	/5	* Name of concerts	/5	* Name trains and busses	/5
* Cut out individually	/5	* Dates and times in target language	/5	* Dates and times in target country language	/5
Total points	/25	**Total points**	/25	**Total points**	/25

Create a Program for a Concert		Create a Train or Bus Schedule	
* 8.5 x 11 in., folded	/5	* Each schedule 8.5 x 11 in., folded	/5
* Illustrated front cover in color with title of event, date, and time	/5	* Include departures and destinations	/5
* List of target country performers	/5	* Min. 1 graphic/illustration	/5
* Use target language	/5	* Include times and days	/5
* Neatly written and drawn or computer generated	/5	* Neatly written or computer generated in target language	/5
Total points	/25	**Total points**	/25

Show your project choices to your teacher by: _____

All of your projects are due on: _____

Vacation and Travel

Complete one from Column I and one more from Columns II or III.

Column I	Column II	Column III
Create a Diorama Pick a place to "visit" in the target country and create a diorama with labels.	**You are the Tour Guide** Pretend you are a tour guide in a major city in the target country. Create a PowerPoint speech in the target language.	**Design a Brochure** Design a brochure for your travel destination in the target country.
Create a Quiz and a Worksheet Create a quiz and a worksheet with vacation and travel vocabulary.	**Create a Pop-Up Book** Create a pop-up book of travel destinations in the target country.	**Write an Article** Write an article for a travel magazine (e.g. NGS Traveler, Condé Nast, etc.) about a target country destination.
Illustrate a Packing List Illustrate and label a packing list as you pack for a trip to the target country.	**Compare and Contrast** You are traveling to the target country. Compare and contrast your packing list with that of someone traveling to your native country.	**Give a Persuasive Speech** Give a persuasive speech on the benefits of traveling to the target country or city.

- **Challenge 1**: Interview a Person from the Target Country. Find a person from the target country and interview him/her about traveling to his/her homeland.
- **Challenge 2**: Create a Complete Travel Itinerary for a two-week trip to the target country. Include dates, days of the week, and a different activity for each day.

Interview a Person from the Target Country		Create a Complete Travel Itinerary	
* Include name, phone or e-mail address for teacher review	___ / 5	* Two week timespan	___ / 5
* Min. 10 questions	___ / 5	* Dates and days of week	___ / 5
* Must be in target language	___ / 5	* Different site or activity for each day	___ / 5
* Videotape or record interview	___ / 5	* Complete sentences	___ / 5
* Share with class	___ / 5	* Include transportation and accommodations	___ / 5
Total points	___ / 25	**Total points**	___ / 25

Differentiated Instruction for World Languages ©2013 Hubbert and Nieminen

Vacation and Travel Assessment Rubric

Column I	Column II	Column III
Create a Diorama	**You are the Tour Guide**	**Design a Brochure**
* Min. 1 shoebox size (or approx. 5x14x16) ___/5	* 10 content slides ___/5	* 8.5 x 11 in., folded ___/5
* Min. five 3-D objects ___/5	* Title slide with student name ___/5	* Must be factual and in the target language ___/5
* All surfaces decorated ___/5	* Graphic(s) and words on each slide ___/5	* Illustrations in color ___/5
* Title your diorama ___/5	* Monologue written out ___/5	* Use complete sentences ___/5
* Must be in target language ___/5	* Present to class ___/5	* Neatly written or computer generated ___/5
Total points ___/25	**Total points ___/25**	**Total Points ___/25**
Create a Quiz and a Worksheet	**Create a Pop-Up Book**	**Write an Article**
* 8.5 x 11 in. ___/5	* 5 x 7 in., bound ___/5	* 2-3 paragraphs ___/5
* Use vacation/ travel vocabulary ___/5	* Min. 5 pop-up pages ___/5	* Typed, double-spaced, max. size 14 font ___/5
* Creative design ___/5	* Must be in color and in the target language ___/5	* Location must be in target country ___/5
* Neatly written or computer generated ___/5	* Illustrated front cover with title and student name ___/5	* Photo(s) in color with caption(s) ___/5
* Answer key included ___/5	* Location with descriptions included ___/5	* Correct grammar and spelling ___/5
Total points ___/25	**Total points ___/25**	**Total points ___/25**
Illustrate a Packing List	**Compare and Contrast**	**Give a Persuasive Speech**
* 8.5 x 11 in. ___/5	* Make a list for each person in the target language ___/5	* 1-2 minutes ___/5
* Min. 10 items in the target language ___/5	* Min. 10 items each ___/5	* Must have persuasive elements ___/5
* Label each color illustration ___/5	* Min. 2 illustrations per list ___/5	* Typed script to teacher prior to presentation ___/5
* Include target country name in the title of the list ___/5	* Compare in a Venn diagram or a paragraph ___/5	* Min. 2 visual aids ___/5
* Neatly written or computer generated ___/5	* Label Venn, title paragraph ___/5	* Perform with adequate volume ___/5
Total points ___/25	**Total points ___/25**	**Total points ___/25**

Show your project choices to your teacher by: _____

All of your projects are due on: _____

Visiting or Obtaining Services from Community Service Programs ~ Teacher's Choice

English	Target Language
Map Out the Embassy Find out your home country embassy's address, phone number, and other contact information in the target country. Draw a map from your "hotel" to the embassy.	**What to Do?** Pretend that no one can understand your native language, and that you must explain your problem to him/her. Choose 3: ➢ Injury (talk to doctor) ➢ Toothache (talk to dentist) ➢ Fire (talk to fireman on the phone) ➢ Accident (talk to police) ➢ Lost (ask a policeman for directions)
Compare and Contrast Professions Compare and contrast professions between the target country and your country. Include the following: ✓ Training and Education ✓ Duties and Responsibilities ✓ Salaries ✓ Hours of work ✓ Vacation time	**Compare Facilities** Compare medical facilities, police and fire stations, etc. in the target country and in your country.
Uniform Research Research uniforms or attire for the following professions in the target country: ❖ Doctor ❖ Dentist ❖ Police ❖ Fire You may display your work in illustrated form or by using a PowerPoint presentation.	**Write and Illustrate a Children's Book** Write and illustrate a children's book about going to the dentist or doctor or visiting a police or fire station. 

Visiting or Obtaining Services from Community Service Programs Assessment Rubric

English | Target Language

Map Out the Embassy

* Include address, phone number, and contact information for the embassy	____/5
* Web page name and URL	____/5
* Pick a real hotel to "stay" at	____/5
* Map must be in color and to scale	____/5
* Map key and compass rose on map	____/5
Total points	____/25

What to Do?

* Min. 4 sentences for each choice	____/5
* Content is relevant and in target language	____/5
* Neatly written or typed	____/5
* Correct pronunciation	____/5
* Present to class with a partner	____/5
Total points	____/25

Compare and Contrast Professions

* 8.5 x 11 in. sheet for each profession	____/5
* Compare min. of 3 professions	____/5
* Separate paragraph or Venn, with separate titles for each profession	____/5
* Neatly written and/or drawn	____/5
* All required information included	____/5
Total points	____/25

Compare Facilities

* Select 3 facilities	____/5
* List 3 similarities and 3 differences per choice	____/5
* Min. 1 illustration per choice	____/5
* Must be in target language	____/5
* Display your results creatively	____/5
Total points	____/25

Uniform Research

* 8.5 x 11 in. or 5 slides each profession	____/5
* Each profession included	____/5
* Illustrations must be in color	____/5
* Write short description for each uniform/attire	____/5
* Use complete sentences in descriptions	____/5
Total points	____/25

Write and Illustrate a Children's Book

* Min. 5 x7 in., bound, 10 pages min.	____/5
* Must be in target language	____/5
* Neatly written and drawn or computer generated with color illustrations	____/5
* Title page with author name	____/5
* Read to class	____/5
Total points	____/25

Show your project choices to your teacher by: _____

All of your projects are due on: _____

Teacher Tips for Pages 97-103

Standards

Shopping				Eating Out			
All projects				All projects			
2.2				1.3	2.1	2.2	3.2

Public and Private Schools

4.2	1.3	4.2
4.2	3.1/Tech	1.3
3.2	1.3	

- ❖ **Preview Material**
    - o For videotaped or recorded products, it is always wise to preview the video or recording prior to class presentation.
- ❖ **Shopping**
    - o If possible, take students on a field trip to an ethnic store in your area. Write out a pretend shopping list: assign students to find items in the store, have students find prices for certain items, and then compare online pricing of the same item.
- ❖ **Eating Out**
    - o Have students plan an ethnic dinner for the entire class. The students need to create a menu and a shopping list as well as dish assignments for each student group (e.g. Group 1 makes appetizers, group 2 makes the entrée, group 3 the dessert, and group 4 provides beverages).
    - o Take your student group to an ethnic restaurant.
- ❖ **Public and Private Schools**
    - o This is a Teacher's Choice. See page 34 for instructions on Teacher's Choice.
    - o Ask exchange students in your school to give presentations about their school systems.

Shopping Experience

Shopping Rules:
1. Choose a shopping experience.
2. Then choose an appropriate project to complete for that shopping experience.
3. Use target language in all projects.
4. Show your choices to your teacher by:_____.
5. Your project(s) are due: _____.

Shopping Experience

- Clothing
- Personal Items
- Food
- Entertainment
- Sports/Fitness Equipment
- Hobbies
- Dishes
- School Supplies
- Music
- Automobile items or gas

Project

- ❖ Create a Scrapbook
- ❖ Buy Holiday Items
- ❖ Plan a Party

- ❖ Create a Shopping List
- ❖ Create an Online Ad (e.g. E-bay)
- ❖ Create an Advertisement

- ❖ Design a Sales Flyer
- ❖ Create the Front Page of an "Online" Store
- ❖ Craft a Diorama

- ❖ Create a Poster or Collage of Items from a Store
- ❖ Draw a Map of Store Locations in a target country or city
- ❖ Draw a Store Front with Large Display Windows

Differentiated Instruction for World Languages ©2013 Hubbert and Nieminen

Shopping Experience Assessment Rubric

Create a Scrapbook		Buy Holiday Items		Plan a Party	
* Min. 5 pages	___/5	* Choose 10 items to "purchase"	___/5	* Make a shopping list of 10 items	___/5
* Min. 3 pictures on each page	___/5	* Include prices for each	___/5	* Party must have a theme and a purpose	___/5
* Must be in color	___/5	* Label each item	___/5	* Display cost of party	___/5
* Label pictures with prices	___/5	*Display items creatively	___/5	* Create an invitation	___/5
* Cover with title and student name	___/5	* Present to class	___/5	* List 3 activities to do at the party	___/5
Total points	___/25	**Total points**	___/25	**Total Points**	___/25

Create a Shopping List		Create an Online Ad		Create an Advertisement	
* 8.5 x 11 in.	___/5	* 5 items with prices	___/5	* 8.5 x 11 in.	___/5
* 25 items	___/5	* Must be in color	___/5	* Prices for each item	___/5
* Prices for all items with total amount spent	___/5	* Use technology terms such as "add to cart"	___/5	* Illustration in color for each item	___/5
* Organize by category	___/5	* Description of each item	___/5	* Create a catch phrase	___/5
* Neatly written or typed with border or background	___/5	* Neatly written and typed or computer generated	___/5	* Neatly written and drawn or computer generated	___/5
Total points	___/25	**Total points**	___/25	**Total Points**	___/25

Design a Sales Flyer		Create the Front Page		Craft a Diorama	
* 8.5 x 11 in.	___/5	* Include store name and catch phrase	___/5	* Min. 1 shoebox size (or approx. 5x14x16)	___/5
* Min. 5 items	___/5	* Website format ; tabs for e.g. sales, categories, etc.	___/5	* Store name as title	___/5
* Include original and sale prices	___/5	* Feature sale item of the week	___/5	* Must be actual target country store	___/5
* Illustrations in color	___/5	* Must use target language	___/5	* Min. five 3-D objects	___/5
* Include store name and date(s) of sale	___/5	* Neatly written and drawn or computer generated	___/5	* All surfaces must be decorated	___/5
Total points	___/25	**Total points**	___/25	**Total points**	___/25

Create a Poster or Collage		Draw a Map of Stores		Draw a Store Front	
* Standard poster size	___/5	* Min. 10 locations	___/5	* 12 x 18 in.	___/5
* Min. 15 items	___/5	* Shopping center = 1 store	___/5	* Min. 15 items	___/5
* Label each item (collage labels can be on reverse)	___/5	* Label with store names and addresses	___/5	* Items in window can be photos, cut-outs, or drawn	___/5
* Illustrations in color	___/5	* Illustrate in color	___/5	* Must be in color	___/5
* Title poster or collage	___/5	* Include map key and compass	___/5	* Store name in target language	___/5
Total points	___/25	**Total points**	___/25	**Total points**	___/25

Eating Out

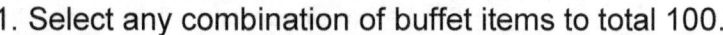

Score 100 ~ Choose from the Buffet
1. Select any combination of buffet items to total 100.
2. Mark your choices and show your teacher by: _____.
3. All projects are due by: _____.

Appetizers 20

- Make a Crossword Puzzle with target vocabulary.
- Make a Reservation at two different restaurants.
- Write out a Recipe Card of menu items.
- Survey and Graph your classmates' favorite ethnic restaurants.

Beverages 30

- Identify Fast Food Restaurants in the target country.
- Draw and Label a Floor Plan of a restaurant.
- Research an Ethnic Restaurant from the target country located in your country.
- Your Choice!

Side Dishes 50

- Write and Perform a Skit about restaurants in the target country.
- Prepare a Dish from a real restaurant in the target country by researching their menus.
- Design a Placemat that fits a real restaurant's atmosphere.
- Your Choice!

Entrees 80

- Videotape a Commercial for a restaurant in the target country.
- Design a Mural for an ethnic, target country restaurant.
- Write a Theme Song for an ethnic restaurant.
- Your Choice!

Desserts 100

- Create and Design a Board Game using restaurant/food vocabulary.
- Write a Critique of your favorite ethnic restaurant.
- Create a Pretend "Website" for your favorite ethnic restaurant.
- Your Choice!

Differentiated Instruction for World Languages ©2013 Hubbert and Nieminen

Eating Out Assessment Rubric

Make a Crossword Puzzle	
* 20 words	____/5
* Appropriate clues	____/5
* Solution in target language	____/5
* Neatly written or computer generated	____/5
* Provide puzzle with answer key	____/5
Total points	____/25

Make a Reservation	
* Each dialogue with 5 lines in target language	____/5
* Written or typed script	____/5
* Correct grammar and structure	____/5
* Correct pronunciation	____/5
* Perform with a partner	____/5
Total points	____/25

Write Out a Recipe Card	
* Min. 5 x 7 in.	____/5
* Name of dish	____/5
* List of ingredients	____/5
* Numbered steps	____/5
* Neatly written or typed in the target language	____/5
Total points	____/25

Survey and Graph	
* Survey 10 classmates	____/5
* Ask questions in target language	____/5
* Title graph with axes labeled	____/5
* Graph in color	____/5
* Include original tally sheet	____/5
Total points	____/25

Identify Fast Food Restaurants	
* List names of restaurants	____/5
* Describe each restaurant in complete sentences	____/5
* List the types of food served	____/5
* Include some menu items with prices	____/5
* Neatly written or typed in the target language	____/5
Total points	____/25

Draw and Label a Floor Plan	
* Min. 8.5 x 11 in.	____/5
* Include all essential areas of a restaurant	____/5
* Use color	____/5
* Label areas and items correctly in the target language	____/5
* Include a title for your work	____/5
Total points	____/25

Research an Ethnic Restaurant	
* Name and location of restaurant	____/5
* Min. 10 menu items served, use the target language	____/5
* Display data creatively	____/5
* Use color effectively	____/5
* Share info with class	____/5
Total points	____/25

Write and Perform a Skit	
* 2-5 minutes in length, in target language	____/5
* Min. 3 restaurants	____/5
* Include props and costumes	____/5
* Copy of written dialogue with stage directions to teacher for review	____/5
* Perform skit	____/5
Total points	____/25

Prepare a Dish	
* Must be an ethnic dish	____/5
* Include recipe	____/5
* Turn in research	____/5
* Photograph your prepared dish	____/5
* Prepare dish and serve it to the class	____/5
Total points	____/25

Design a Placemat	
* 12 x 18 in.	____/5
* Include name of restaurant	____/5
* Illustrations in color, must include border	____/5
* Include both pictures and words	____/5
* All words must be in target language	____/5
Total points	____/25

Assessments continue on the next page

Eating Out Assessment Rubric

Videotape a Commercial		Design a Mural	
* 30-60 seconds long	/5	* Min. 24 x 54 in. (= six 12 x 18 sheets of construction paper)	/5
* Script to teacher for review	/5	* 15 illustrations	/5
* Must be in target language	/5	* Neatly drawn or painted	/5
* Include props and costume(s)	/5	* Must be in color	/5
* Perform live or play video	/5	* Display in classroom	/5
Total points	/25	**Total points**	/25

Write a Theme Song		Create and Design a Board Game	
* 1-2 minutes long, use target language	/5	* Min. 11 x17 in. (open file folder)	/5
* Must have melody	/5	* 20 question/vocabulary cards in the target language	/5
* Title your song	/5	* Thematic title and background	/5
* Written words for teacher review	/5	* Must be in color	/5
* Perform live or play recording	/5	* Clear set of rules and directions	/5
Total points	/25	**Total points**	/25

Write a Critique		Create a Pretend "Website"	
* 1-3 paragraphs	/5	* Website format ; tabs for menu & location, etc.	/5
* Cover food selection and service	/5	* Creative name and URL	/5
* Title and student name	/5	* Neatly written and drawn or computer generated, use target language	/5
* Typed, double-spaced, max. size 14 font	/5	* Graphics enhance "website"	/5
* Must include one picture with caption	/5	* Must be in color	/5
Total points	/25	**Total points**	/25

_____!		_____!	
	/5		/5
	/5		/5
	/5		/5
	/5		/5
	/5		/5
Total points	/25	**Total points**	/25

Public and Private Schools ~ Teacher's Choice

- Write a Review about the target country's school system. Include funding, classes, teachers, administration, etc.

- Design a Brochure for a school/university in the target country. May be fictional.

- Fill out a Typical School Schedule for your grade in the target country Use the target language.

- Research High School Graduation Requirements in the target country and share your results creatively.

- Produce a Videotaped Ad for a school in the target country.

- Draw a Storyboard illustrating "A Day in the Life of…" a middle school/high school student in the target country.

- Make a Collage of classes, activities, logo, motto, etc. of a public or private school or a university in the target country.

- Create a Pretend Facebook Page for a class, school or university in the target country.

Public and Private Schools Assessment Rubric

Write a Review		Design a Brochure		Fill Out a Typical School Schedule	
* 1-3 paragraphs	____/5	* 8.5 x 11 in., folded	____/5	* 8.5 x 11 in	____/5
*Typed, double-spaced, max. size 14 font	____/5	* Use both pictures and words	____/5	* In table format, may be computer generated	____/5
* Title includes name of target country	____/5	* Name of school and graphic on front page	____/5	* Include all school days	____/5
* Min. 1 graphic with caption	____/5	* Include address and contact info	____/5	* Include all classes attended each day	____/5
* Include all required information	____/5	* Neatly written or computer generated	____/5	* Include lunch and after-school clubs	____/5
Total points	____/25	**Total points**	____/25	**Total Points**	____/25

Research High School Graduation Requirements		Produce a Videotaped Ad		Draw a Storyboard	
* Include information about graduation ceremony	____/5	* 1-2 minutes long	____/5	* 12 x 18 in	____/5
* Discuss final/exit exams	____/5	* Include visual	____/5	*. Min. 6-8 squares	____/5
* Turn in research	____/5	* Include props and costume(s)	____/5	* Picture with words in each square	____/5
* Display and share results creatively	____/5	* Script turned in for teacher review prior to performance	____/5	* Illustrations in color	____/5
* Present to class	____/5	* Present videotaped performance	____/5	* Title with student name in first square	____/5
Total points	____/25	**Total points**	____/25	**Total points**	____/25

Make a Collage		Create a Pretend Facebook Page	
* 12 x 18 in.	____/5	* Creative title for the page	____/5
* Min. 10 items	____/5	* Use Facebook template	____/5
* Illustrations in color (drawings, magazine or internet pictures)	____/5	* Use target language	____/5
* Include classes and activities	____/5	* Use complete sentences in the comments	____/5
* Include logo and motto	____/5	* Include min. 5 "posts"	____/5
Total points	____/25	**Total points**	____/25

Show your project choices to your teacher by: _____

All of your projects are due on: _____

Reference Pages and Templates

- ❖ Teacher Tips for Pages 106-114 105
- ❖ Shopping List 106
- ❖ Facts and Figures 107
- ❖ Commands 108
- ❖ Clock template 109
- ❖ Facebook Page template 110
- ❖ Race for the Numbers 112
- ❖ Bingo Chart template 113
- ❖ More Verb Activities 114

Teacher Tips for Pages 106-114

- ❖ **Shopping List**
    - o Make copies, distribute to students and parents, and ask for donations.

- ❖ **Facts and Figures**
    - o Copy page for each student or group
    - o Assign 5-10 items from the lists and choose medium OR
    - o Instruct student(s) to choose from lists: e.g. 5-10 items to display on a product of their choice
    - o Have students create media products using all of the listed facts and figures

- ❖ **Commands**
    - o Students never see the commands written. This is a Total Physical Response (TPR) activity. Students only hear and do the commands!
        1. The teacher must model each command when it is first introduced; students imitate the teacher.
        2. Only introduce two to four new commands each day.
        3. Previously learned commands should be reviewed daily for optimal student retention.

- ❖ **Clock template**
    - o Tip: enlarge template before making copies
    - **Supplies you will need:**
    - o Two colors of construction paper, brass paper fasteners, glue, and scissors.
    - o Use heavy paper or cardstock to copy clock face and hands, or have students glue onto construction paper. Cut out the hands.
    - o Make a small hole in the center of the clock's face and one in each of the clock's hands. Using the brass paper fastener, attach the hands to the clock.

- ❖ **Facebook**
    - o 1st empty space (rectangle): First Name
    - o 2nd empty space (small square): Photo
    - o 3rd empty space (rectangle): Full Name
    - o Then fill in "Status" and "Comments"

- ❖ **Bingo Chart Template**
    - o Students draw pictures of vocabulary words to use as bingo charts.

- ❖ **More Verb Activities**
    - o A list of extra activities to use with verbs.

Shopping List

- Poster board
- Markers
- Colored pencils
- White copy paper
- 8.5 x 11 and 12 x 18 construction paper
- Scissors
- Old magazines
- Magazines in the target language
- Yarn/string
- Glue
- Tape
- Paper fasteners/brads
- Paper punch
- Rulers
-
-
-

Non-essential, but beneficial
- Magnetic strip
- Glitter glue
- Glue gun
-
-

Facts and Figures

The two lists below depict the most common "facts and figures" categories for any target country you are studying. To understand the culture and the language of a country, you should be familiar with the items on these lists. They are also an easy reference for you to make a poster of the target country's facts and figures.

- Currency
- Population
- Language(s) spoken
- Capital and major cities
- History and historical dates
- Types of ethnicities/holidays/celebrations
- Principal products
- Natural resources
- Economy: agriculture and industry
- Imports and exports
- Geography and physical features
- Making a living/median wage
- Foods
- Government

- Nature: animals and plants
- Climate: seasons and weather
- Places of interest and historical sites
- Sports: national and international
- Transportation
- Education: public and private
- Map: outline, latitude, longitude
- Military: types and service
- National flag, anthem, motto, symbols, crest, etc.
- Communication and technology
- Religion(s)
- Family life

Commands

1. Stand up. Sit down.
2. Raise your right hand.
3. Raise your left hand.
4. Put your hands over your head, over the book, pencil, stapler, etc.
5. Touch your nose.
6. Touch the desk.
7. Touch the floor.
8. Touch another person's desk.
9. Touch the board.
10. Touch the teacher's desk.
11. Open the door.
12. Close the door.
13. Open the window, curtain, cupboard, etc.
14. Close the window, curtain, cupboard, etc.
15. Turn on the lights.
16. Turn off the lights.
17. Sit down.
18. Sit in another chair/desk.
19. Sit in the teacher's chair.
20. Sit on the floor.
21. Come here.
22. Put your pencil on the floor.
23. Pick up the pencil on the floor.
24. Turn around.
25. Turn to the right.
26. Turn to the left.
27. Trade seats with another person.
28. Trade pencils with another person.
29. Trade books with another person.
30. Throw away paper.
31. Write your name on the board.
32. Write the numbers 1-10 on the board.
33. Draw a big circle on the board.
34. Draw a house in the circle.
35. Draw a tree in the circle.
36. Erase the board.
37. Erase the house in the circle.
38. Shake hands with another person/teacher.
39. Bark like a dog.
40. Shout "Look at me!"
41. Walk around your desk, the teacher's desk.
42. Jump up and down.
43. Jump over the paper on the floor.
44. Say "hi" to another person.
45. Tell me your birthday.
46. Make a basket. (Nerf ball and net) ☺
47. Bring me your pencil.
48. Walk to the teacher's desk.
49. Write "THE" on the board.
50. Write "END" on the board.

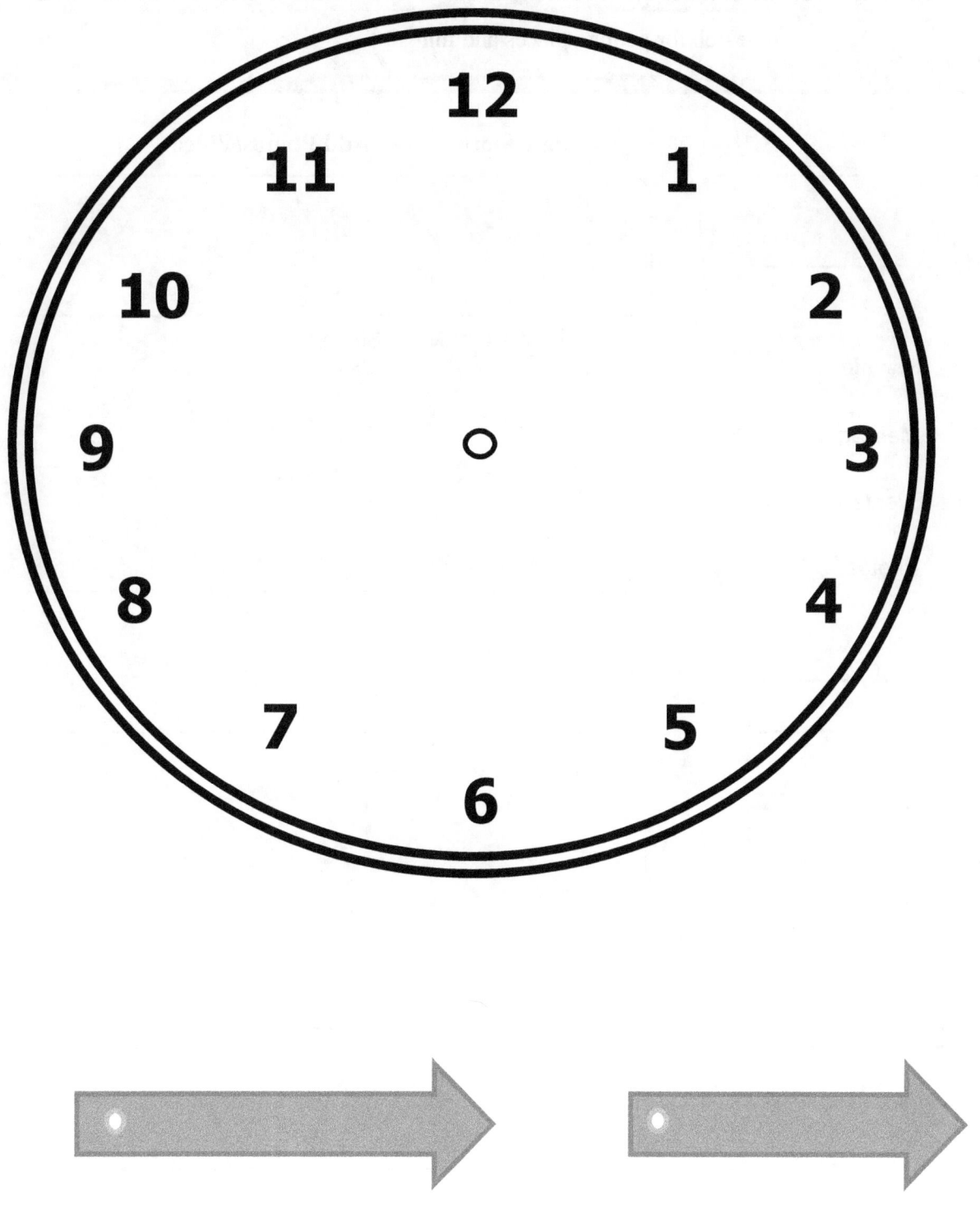

- Glue onto construction paper. Cut out the hands.
- Make a small hole in the center of the clock's face and one in each of the clock's hands. Using the brass paper fastener, attach the hands to the clock.

facebook

Search for people, places and things

Home

☐ Update Status   Add Photos/Video

Newsfeed

Messages

Events

Photos

Groups

Apps

Like · Comment · Share ·

Like · Comment · Share ·

Like · Comment · Share ·

☐ **Update Status**   Add Photos/Video

Like · Comment · Share ·

Like · Comment · Share ·

Like · Comment · Share ·

Race for the Numbers

<u>Instructions for the Game:</u>

The object of the game is to see who can identify the selected number on the board the fastest.

1. Arabic numerals 1-100 are written randomly on the white-board with a black marker.
2. The class is divided into two teams. Each team is assigned a "color" by the teacher depending on the color availability of the marker selection. ☺
3. Choose one person to be the "fixer." This person's job is to erase any incorrectly circled number and to re-write the number in its original form. Reminder: The fixer uses a black marker!
4. The teacher calls out a number in the target language.
5. One person from each team races to the board to find the number. When they find it, they must circle it with a marker. (Each team *must* use their assigned colored marker to circle the numbers!)
6. If the wrong number is circled, continue play until the *correct* number is circled.
7. However, if neither player circles the *correct* number within a teacher-determined time limit, the number is discarded.
8. The winning team is the one that has identified the most numbers *correctly*.

<u>Timesaving Teacher Tips:</u>

❖ Teacher selects team captains who then select their teams. Each captain assigns playing order for team members (first, second, third, etc.)

❖ Make (or have students make) a set of cards with numbers 1-100. Use those numbers to select from - this also ensures that each number is only called once. You can also use the cards to keep track of scoring in the following way:
   1. Assign colors for the teams based on your marker-color selection as mentioned above.
   2. Lay corresponding pieces of colored construction paper on either side of you.
   3. When a team gets a point, lay the number on its corresponding colored paper.

❖ Instead of having to write the numbers on the board each time you play the game, write the numbers on index cards, laminate them, and then affix a short strip of magnetic tape on the back. Students can then identify the numbers by drawing an X or / on the card with their marker.

By Sue Hubbert

More Verb Activities

- ❖ Make flashcards of verb vocabulary.
- ❖ Make a flipbook using verb vocabulary.
- ❖ Draw a cartoon/comic using verbs vocabulary.
- ❖ Create a word search with target vocabulary.
- ❖ Create a children's book of verbs.
- ❖ Write simple sentences about professions using action verbs.
- ❖ Make a scrapbook of 15 verbs using different tenses.
- ❖ Make a game of commands using verb vocabulary.
- ❖ Survey classmates about their weekend activities; translate their answers into target language or use target language throughout survey.
- ❖ Create a crossword puzzle where the solution word is a verb.
- ❖ Choose a famous person to role play from the target country. Describe 10 activities you can/would do if you were that person.

Notes:

www.ingramcontent.com/pod-product-compliance
Lightning Source LLC
Chambersburg PA
CBHW081422230426
43668CB00016B/2323